Is Real Love Worth My Life?

D M Cummings

Also by D M Cummings

Diamond's Pearl
Take a walk in my Shoes

Coming March 2023

I cried…but I never GAVE UP

The World Is Mine (TWIM) Publishing
P.O. Box 3086
Akron, OH 44309

This book is a work of fiction. Names characters, places and incidents are products of the author's imagination or are used fictitiously. Any resemblance to actual events, locales or persons, living or dead, is coincidental.

Copyright @ 2005 by D M Cummings

Revised 2023

All rights reserved,
Including the right of reproduction
in whole or in part in any form.

ISBN: 0-9773854-0-X
9780977385409

Cover designed by A P Bolden
Manufactured in the United States of America

INTRODUCTION

It's been almost 10 years since Mike and I met and I'll be damned if I let his six old baby mamas', his two new baby mama's or a few ass whippings here or there tear us apart. He owes me; I've given up everything for him, the love of my life, my dream of having a family, not just a baby daddy, and basically my life. I've given him everything that he's asked for even a pretty, little girl, even though it jeopardized my relationship with my friends and family.

I learned how to live with his other women and the smacks in the mouth when I asked about them. The lies all became reality. The kids coming out of the woodwork became my kids. My friends distanced themselves from me because every time we went out he would bust out my car windows or we would be fighting. I still stayed with him when he slashed two of my tires and left me in the roughest projects in Akron in the middle of the night when I was four months pregnant. But through all of this, he was there for me in my time of need, he showed me love and gave me sexual healing. Although we weren't married, Mike was in it for the long run, until death do us part. He's going to repay me with his life for all the blood, all the tears, every headache, heartbreak, all the love that I have given him and the ten years that I did nothing but catered to his ass, or is it worth it?

DEDICATION

This book is dedicated to the late Jamesetta (Jamie) Antoine, you are gone and now in a better place and you will never be forgotten.

Rest in Paradise baby girl.
October 1, 1976 – January 14, 2005

ACKNOWLEDGEMENTS

I would like to thank God for helping me get through the obstacles that life has given me, without him there's no telling where I would be. To my mom and dad, thanks for bring me into this world, for your encouraging words, your support and for believing in me, now maybe I can spoil you'll like you have done me. To my daughter thanks for being patient when I had to take time to take care of me, even though there were times when I was frustrated because I couldn't get things to go my way, you understood, and I'll make it up to you. And to my homeboys Jamie Johnson and Tony Jackson, thank you both for listening when I needed to vent and for your good ideas and encouraging words.

INTRODUCTION

It's been almost 10 years since Mike and I met and I'll be damned if I let his six old baby mamas', his two new baby mama's or a few ass whippings here or there tear us apart. He owes me; I've given up everything for him, the love of my life, my dream of having a family, not just a baby daddy, and basically my life. I've given him everything that he's asked for even a pretty, little girl, even though it jeopardized my relationship with my friends and family.

I learned how to live with his other women and the smacks in the mouth when I asked him about them. The lies all became reality. The kids coming out of the woodwork became my kids. My friends distanced themselves from me because every time we went out, he would bust out my car windows or we would be fighting, but I still stayed with him when he slashed two of my tires and left me in the roughest projects in Akron in the middle of the night when I was four months pregnant. But through all of this, he was there for me in my time of need, he showed me love and gave me sexual healing. Although we weren't married, Mike was in it for the long run, until death do us part. He's going to repay me with his life for all the blood, all the tears, every headache, heartbreak, all the love that I have given him and the ten years that I did nothing but catered to his ass or is it worth it?

CHAPTER- 1

I'm lying across my bed looking at the ceiling, thanking God for my health and well-being. I'm so lucky to be alive and able to write this book. I have made some very selfish and immature decisions that could have cost me my life.

Growing up I developed a negative attitude about life. My parents divorced when I was young and I watched my mom struggle to try to make sure her three kids had everything they wanted and needed, if necessary, and as I got older, I found a way to get things on my own. I wasn't one of those kids born with a silver spoon in their mouths, but I lived comfortably, and I felt that I should be able to have anything or anybody that I wanted because that's how life had been to me. I had my heart broken many times in the past, which only made me stronger. Shortly after my parents divorced, when I was in the fourth grade, my dad walked out of our lives. He would take us skating on Saturday mornings, but after a while that stopped. I would call him and that was the only way that we talked, so I began to look up to my older brother Cleo, he was four years older than I, and he took the time out for me and kept me up to date on how men were and that they only wanted to get some tail. But he went to the Military when I was fifteen, then he was sent to Desert Storm, so I didn't have anyone. My mom was there, but she was mostly at work, and it wasn't the same. Then this guy tried to take my goodies. My girls and I would always wrestle in the hallways with the boys, this particular, day I had on a skirt. Travis, this boy at my school ran up behind me and tried to slam me on the ground, but he couldn't get me down.
"Stop Travis, I quit."
"Alright, alright." He acted like he was walking away and then he ran over and picked me up over his shoulder. I started screaming and grabbing the back of my skirt, so my panties wouldn't show. He carried me into the girl's locker room.

"You are going to get in trouble; you better get out of here." He started laughing and carried me all the way to the stairway that led to the gym where he put me down. The only way I knew to get out was back the way I came because the gym doors were locked. I started up the steps and he grabbed my leg and I fell. I tried to kick him, but he grabbed my leg again and reached his hand under my skirt and grabbed a hold of my panties.

"Get off me! Man, I'm not playing no more." I started pulling myself up the stairs, but he was pulling me back by my panties and then I felt them rip. A big lump appeared in my throat and my eyes filled with tears. "Travis, why are you playing?"

"Don't try to act like you don't want it, you wore this little bitty skirt for something." I continued to pull away from him, and then I felt his finger touch my vagina. He had let my leg go so now I had some leverage. I turned around and hit him with my gym bag, which also contained my books, as hard as I could. I was further down the steps, and I could now see an Exit sign, so I knew there had to be a way out somewhere back there. I grabbed my gym bag, and he started trying to pull it away from me and that's when I noticed his penis hanging out. I let the bag go and took off running towards the exit sign, I found the door and I ran out of it. From that day forward my demeanor about men was different. I dated a few guys here and there, but they didn't really mean that much to me. We would talk on the phone or meet at the park, but they never knew where I lived or that much about me because I didn't trust them.

One Saturday afternoon I was with my best friend Tye, over her boyfriend Eric's house, and didn't want to catch the bus, so his boy Otis offered to give us a ride. He was so nice and very attractive, and he appeared to have a lot of intelligence. He was kind of a mama's boy and very spoiled, but so was I, so I could deal with that. He was 5' 9" light skinned with an athletes built. He was driving a nice, newer model blazer, he was dressed nice, had on clean shoes, had pretty, white teeth and he smelt wonderful. We exchanged numbers and after a couple of phone conversations, dinner and a movie he had my nose wide open.

****

It was the middle of my senior year in High School, and I basically thought I was the shit. I was tall about 5'6 1/2", 120 pounds with long jet-black hair. I had a lot of guys trying to get with me and I was very popular. I was always on the merit roll, I was one of the few girls that had never slept with anyone at our school, I had a little hoopty, but it got me from A to B, I had a decent job and one of the finest guys in school. Everything was in my favor. Everyone always considered me as a player because I always had a bunch of guys up under me, but I always had one main dude who I gave one hundred and fifty percent to and at this time it was Otis. Otis and I had been dating for about seven months, he didn't attend East High as I did; he went to St. Vincent. I never got serious with anyone at my school, I been there, done that and it's always some hater that stays in your business and try to keep a bunch of mess going. I knew that I had a bunch of male friends, and I didn't want any problems. I always wore Otis's football jacket with his name on the back to school and every event, dance or whatever we had he was there, and everyone knew he was my number one.

Otis was quiet and pretty much kept to himself, he was also very smart in school and gave one hundred and seventy percent to his woman, although he was really spoiled and kind of a momma's boy, I loved his ass to death. He had a nice ride, was fine as hell and he wasn't conceded. This was my type of guy; we did everything together and this was the man that I wanted to start my family with.

Otis and I usually didn't go anywhere without each other, but one day Tye's mother, was getting married and they had an after party. Otis had basketball practice and couldn't make it, so my other girl Shawn went with me. She had a three-

month-old daughter who is my goddaughter that she brought with us. I was carrying the baby as we were walking into the house and as we approached the porch, Tye's cousin and her boyfriend Eric were standing there talking. I had hooked Tye and Eric up like a year prior and he and Otis were boys.
"What's up Kya?"
"What's up Eric?" and I gave him a hug.
"Damn" her cousin said.
"Oh, this is my dude, Mike. Mike this is my home girl Kya."
Mike and I shook hands.
"Is that your baby?"
"Naw, this is my girl's daughter."
"Why don't you let her take her and you go for a ride with me" and he looked back at his truck, and it was very nice. It was black with a white rag top; it was kitted out sitting on some fat 20's and he had on this gold necklace with his name on it in 3D with diamond cuts. I was impressed and back in the day I would have seen dollar signs and I would have gotten those digits, but I had a good man, and I wasn't trying to mess that up. Eric gave me this goofy look.
"Naw, I'm going to go in here and holla at my girl and my man probably wouldn't like that, but it was nice meeting you." I walked into the house, said what's up to Tye, congratulated her mother and gave her the card that I had brought for her. We ate, socialized and started dancing. I was always into the music videos, so I knew all the new dances. I was teaching Tye and her mom how to do the butterfly and I was all the way down to the floor. I had my right hand on the floor, and I was working my hips until everybody started laughing. I looked behind me and Mike was standing there with this big grin on his face.
"Why you stop? I'm trying to learn too."
"Tye knows how to do it. Let her show you."
"I can't do that," Tye said.
"Don't act all shy now, show me how to do it," Mike said. I was demonstrating and he was learning, we were all laughing and having a good time. It was this pregnant girl there with this cute

little boy running around the house that was sitting in the living room with my girl Shawn. I thought it was Tye's older sister's friend because she never came out and said anything but when we started dancing and she heard the conversation going on in the kitchen she ran in there and was just staring at me all mean and crazy. We continued to dance for a while then I pulled Tye to the side.
"Who is that?"
"That's Cynthia, one of Mike's baby's moms. That's his son right there," and she pointed to the little boy that was running around.
"Awe he is hot. He was trying to holla at me outside."
"They're not really together, she just be trippin'".
"So, what... are they here together?" She just kind of chuckled.
"Well girl I'm about to get out of here anyway, my baby should be on his way home and he will call as soon as he gets in the door. So, I'll call you later." Shawn and I got into my little Horizon, put the baby in the car seat and headed home.
"Girl did you see ole' dude trying to holla with his girl in the next room?"
"Yeah, we were sitting there talking and she didn't like that shit."
"It wasn't my fault, he hot, but that was a nice whip he was pushin', and did you see all that gold he was rockin?"
"Naw, I was trying to see what they had to eat, but if I were you, I wouldn't fuck with it."
"Girl please, I'm not trying to mess up my good shit. I'm really into Otis and I'm not trying to lose him."
"I hear you." I dropped Shawn and her baby off at her house, went home and called my "Boo". I told him all about the party and about Mike because I figured Eric was going to tell him anyway and I would have preferred he heard it from me, so he wouldn't think that I was trying to hide anything.

****

I had a couple of other run-ins with Mike over the next few months at Tye's house. I would go over his house when he wasn't there to help Tye clean up for him or just to keep her company and have a few beers with her and he would give us a couple of dollars. Otis wasn't fond of this at all, but he wasn't the controlling type he would just say, he didn't like what you were doing and leave it up to you to make your own decisions. "Look Kya, I know you want to help your girl out and get a few extra dollars in your pocket, but I really don't want you around Mike. I know that he likes you and it's not that I don't trust you, but why put yourself in that predicament?" I understood what he was saying but most of the time Mike wasn't there, and I didn't like being home alone until Otis got done with practice or off work because my brother was either at basketball practice himself or running the streets doing his own thing and my mom was always at work. I explained that to Otis and all he said was "just be home by the time I get home." I could deal with that so that's what I did. This went on for a couple of months, by this time Mike was putting, what I thought, was big money in my pocket even when I didn't help Tye clean. I would just go over there, and he would give me fifteen or twenty dollars. I was averaging about fifty or sixty dollars every other week or so for doing nothing, now this was the life, so I thought. I always made it a point to leave when Tye left, although she didn't stay too far, I always said "I had to take her home."

Tye sensed that Mike and I were getting kind of close, so she put word in my ear that he was sleeping with one of her girls that hung out with us occasionally, but she wasn't getting anything from it but a chance to lie on her back. I didn't care anyways because I wasn't sleeping with him, and I had a man. I knew I was wrong for taking his money, but nobody knew but Shawn. I wouldn't dare tell Tye because that was her people and she would have thought that I was trying to use him, which I wasn't because I never asked him for anything.

One evening I was just getting off from work when my pager went off, I didn't recognize the number, so I went to the pay phone and dialed the number.
"Hello?" I recognized Tye's voice right away.
"What up girl? Where you at?"
"Chillin' over here with Mike. What you about to do?"
"Shit, go to the crib. There's nothing else to do."
"Why don't you swing through and have a drink with me."
"Alright, I'll be there in about twenty minutes."
I arrived at Mike's, got out the car and knocked on the door; Mike let me in.
"What's up Kya?"
"Hey" and I walk into the dining room where Tye was sitting drinking a beer; there were some playing cards on the table like they had just finished playing a game.
"What's popin?"
"Nothing. You in on the game?"
"What are ya'll playin'."
"Pat."
"Ya'll gamblin'?"
"Fifty cents a hand."
"Man, I don't have any money to be giving away."
"Here, I got you the first hand." We played a couple of hands of Pity Pat; I gave Tye back her fifty cents after I won the first hand, and we had a couple of beers. Tye left the room and went to use the phone; she came back into the dining room.
"Aye, I gotta go. My mom said I have to come make the baby some bottles." Tye's daughter was about two years old and just as cute as ever. I volunteered to give her a ride.
"I'll take you home, I'm about to get going anyway."
"No, I'll walk because I'm not in a rush."
"Well just stay about five more minutes and I'll let you off at the corner."
"Naw, you know how my mom be trippin, and she's going to call down here and ya'll can just tell her that I left." I gave her the 'what's up' look I kind of tilted my head to the right, wrinkled

my forehead and gave her a hard blink with my shoulders shrugged and both hands out to the side with my palms up. "I'll be back," she said. I sat on the arm of the couch by the door for like ten minutes then I knew she wasn't coming back. It was beginning to get dark, I knew that Otis would be home soon and he would be calling. I called Mike to come lock his door because his screen door locked with a key from the inside. "Hey Mike, I'm about to go."
"What's the rush?"
"Well, it doesn't look like Tye is coming back and it's getting late." He leaned up against me on the couch and kissed me on the lips and I turned my head.
"Don't do that," and he kind of pushed me over the arm of the couch and lay on top of me.
"Aye, this ain't cool. I'm about to go."
"Alright," he said while getting up off me. "You got my number, so why don't you call me?"
I got up off the couch. "I'll see what I can do".
"Okay, I'll talk to you later. Oh, are you broke?" and he felt my pocket.
"I got like ten dollars" and he handed me a twenty. By this time, I was kind of interested in Mike but I was in love with Otis and I wouldn't dream of cheating on my baby. I went right home and called him, I didn't take off my jacket on anything and when he answered the phone a big smile came on my face.
"Hello?"
"Hey baby, I missed you today."
"I missed you too."
"So why don't you come see me?"
"Let me take a shower and I'll be over."
"No need, I'll take care of all that when you get here." Otis came over; we took a long hot bath together and made passionate love in the bathtub. We went into my bedroom, and he made love to me like he never did before. It was like he knew something was wrong and that was the first time we tried to make a baby.

CHAPTER- 2

Tye came to school that Friday very excited. "Mike's having a big party tonight. Why don't you swing through?"
"Alright, I'll be there. What time?"
"About nine."
"It's on." By this time, I was thinking that Tye was trying to set me up to get "fucked" literally by Mike, it always seemed like she wanted to see me get hurt, but I couldn't prove it. I thought I was just tripping because I never trusted females, but she was really cool and acted like she was down for me, so just to be on the safe side I was going to take Otis with me.

****

We had a Pep assembly this particular Friday, so we did our normal thing. Most of my other home girls dated older guys so they had access to the liquor. We would give Tammy five dollars a piece on Thursday after school and she would bring a duffle bag full of forty ounces of Old English, fifths of Madd Dogg 20/20, Banana Red and anything else that we might have requested. We usually got to school early, and we would all meet about 7:20 am because we had to be in our class around 7:30ish because we were all in the Business Classes. We would all share a couple of bottles because we didn't want to be too drunk in that class because it had a lot to do with our future. But when it was over, we would go into the bathroom and each of us into a stall, I usually had two forties of OE and a pint of Madd Dogg for myself. I would drink a forty and half the pint before the assembly and the rest after, that way I'd have a buzz all day, but I wouldn't get sick. All I needed was to get in trouble; everybody thought I was the perfect student. I was so quiet when I got around the teachers; I got good grades and always volunteered to help and I got along with everybody, although I did a lot of wrong, I never got caught. My homeboy Ed, who was my best male friend, and I were one of the biggest weed sellers in the school and we had a real good reputation, so nobody dared to tell on us. I had my regular clientel that I only dealt with, so I wasn't really worried about them telling. We were so slick with it that I couldn't believe it was this easy. Our school was strict, and we weren't allowed to carry book bags, we had to use see through bags, so Ed and I carried pocket protectors and since I basically sold single joints in school, because they were easier to pass off. We would take the plastic ink strips out of the ink pens and you could fit two or three fat joints in there depending on the size. We got pens at our school store ten for a dollar. The pens with the Black tops had three joints in them and they were worth ten dollars, the blue caps had two joints and it was worth five dollars because they weren't as fat and the red caps had one in it and it was worth two or three dollars depending on who you were. They would just come up to me and be like "Kya, let me get one of those black pens" I'd give them a pen and they'd give me ten dollars. I was doing this; I had a pretty decent job through my business class and Mike was giving me money, so I had it going on, as I thought. My savings account was fat, of course Otis knew nothing about my on the side hustles because he was a good boy and he probably would have left me or gave me an ultimatum, to stop or find somebody else because he was a man of choices.

     School was out and I was feeling good, I had put in my four hours at my job. I could go to work with a buzz because I didn't do anything but talk on the phone to my friends. I may have had a document or two to type, but I could type with my eyes closed and we had spell check, so I wasn't worried about any mistakes. Now I was ready to kick it. I went home and called Otis over because he usually got out of practice early on Fridays, we went to Swenson's, got us something to eat and went back to my house and watched a movie. We had our intimate moment and then it was time to go to Mike's party. I hadn't asked him yet, but I knew he wouldn't tell me no.
"So, Otis, what are you doing for the rest of the night?"

"I wanted to be with you."
"Good because I wanted you to go to a party with me."
"Whose party is it?"
"Tye's cousin, Mike. I told her I would swing through for a minute, but I want you to come with me."
"Okay," he didn't look too thrilled, but for some reason I really wanted to go. We rode down to Mike's house in Otis's car because he felt that the man was supposed to drive the woman and I didn't have a problem with that because he had a nice ride. It wasn't that many cars there, so he parked in front of the house. We got out of the car and knocked on the door. Mike came to the door and kind of hesitated before he opened it. I know that he was shocked that I had brought Otis to his house when I knew that he liked me, but I wanted to show him that I had a man, and I was trying to be faithful to him. Otis and I went in and sat on the couch so that we could see in the dining room where everyone else was sitting. We said our hellos and then Mike came into the living room and offered us a drink. I had an E&J and coke and a beer, but Otis didn't want anything. Otis and I sat in the living room having our own conversation listening to music. Mike was mingling with everyone and every now and then he would come into the living room and make sure we didn't need anything, showing us some hospitality, but Otis was acting all funny and giving Mike a bunch of short answers. Finally, Otis was fed up with Mike being so nice to me.
"Kya, I'm ready to go, aren't you?" I smacked my lips.
"We haven't even been here a good hour. Why are you in a rush?"
"I just don't feel comfortable."
"Well, I'm not ready. You can go ahead and leave. I'll have Tye's sister take me home."
"No, I'm not leaving you, we came together, and we are going to leave together." I continued sitting there and Mike came and picked up my glass. "You want another shot?"
"Sure." Then Otis got pissed.

"I just told you I was ready to go, why are you getting another drink?"
"I just told you I wasn't ready yet, why can't you just be patient?" He rolled his eyes at me and had a real mean mug on his face. I knew he was pissed and that pissed me off because he was tripping no reason. I was really having a good time and I would sit up under him and his boys just about every day, even if I didn't want to. I was just happy to be out somewhere away from the house. So now I was ready for him to go home.
"You know what... Mike, hold off on that drink I'll be back." I looked at Otis and kind of rolled my eyes. "Let's go!" We got outside and I was feeling tipsy. I think Mike had given me a glass full of E&J and just a dab of coke. We got in the car and didn't say two words to each other. When we got back to my house we started arguing.
"Why do you feel like you always have to be up under Mike? Do you like him or something?" "If I liked him, do you think I would have invited you over there?"
"Then why do you have an attitude with me because I don't want you over there?"
"It's not so much that you don't want me over there, it's just you always want me to do what you want to do, and I never say anything and the first time I suggest being around my friends you wanna act all brand new." By this time, I was crying.
"I'm just trying to look out for you."
"Well, I'm a grown woman and I can look out for myself. I'll call you if it's not too late when I get back in."
"Where are you going?"
"Back over Mike's to kick it with my girl."
"You know what, you..." he stopped in the middle of his sentence and rolled his eyes at me. I felt his pain, so I started crying even harder, so I hugged and kissed him on the lips.
"I love you baby."
"I love you too," and he wiped my tears. "If you really want to go back to that party you go ahead, just call me as soon as you get in no matter how late, I'll be up." Otis went home, I went in

the bathroom and washed my face, put on some baby lotion and went back over Mike's. When I got there a few of Mike's boys had come through and they were all standing on his closed in porch. "Oh, so you came back," and he started smiling.
I ignored the statement and went into the house. Tye's mom kind of gave me a dirty look.
"Where's Otis?"
"He wanted to go home," I said.
"Um", and she rolled her eyes. I looked at Tye and she shrugged her shoulders like I don't know. I got myself a beer out of the refrigerator. "I got next on the spades game. Tye you ready to whip on them?"
"You know how we do it."
"Ya'll 'bout to get whipped on", said her brother Tommy and everyone started to laugh. Mike comes back into the house, I was standing in the doorway of the kitchen and the dining room, he walked in the dining room where everyone else was sitting and started doing the butterfly. He was really drunk, so he couldn't keep his balance and kind of fell over and everybody started laughing. He came close to where I was standing.
"What are you laughing at?" I just shook my head from side to side.
"Nothing".
He looked at my drink. "Oh, that's all you drinkin' is that beer?" I looked at my beer, which was halfway full. "Let me hook you up, E&J and coke, right?"
"You know it." He handed me a plastic cup; it was so full that the liquor spilled on my hand.
"Who gon' drink all this?" I asked.
"It's just ice, you'll be alright." I took a sip; it wasn't that strong, and I was a drinker so I figured I could handle it.

    They finished their hand of spades, so now it was our turn. I was glad because I was tired of standing and I had a buzz. My cup was still pretty much full, but my beer was almost gone.

Tye had gotten up to go to the bathroom. When she came back, they had already dealt the cards and I had the bomb hand.
"How ya'll play?" I asked because everybody doesn't play the same.
"Ace down, this a real man's game," said Tommy.
"Okay then, get ready to get beat like a real man," I said while laughing. I could talk trash because I had the Ace, King, Jack, 10, 7, and 3 of spades. I also had the Ace of heart, King of diamond and Club. That was seven books of my own, not including what my partner may have had and if you get 10 on the first hand that's an automatic two hundred points and we were only playing to 350. We got twelve books the first hand, so the game was pretty much over.
"Oh, look at that, did we just run a Boston on them?" I'm talking a lot of trash; my drink was about gone, and I was drunk. Everybody looked like they were moving in slow motion, and I had the giggles.
"That was just beginners' luck." Tommy said.
"We can run it again, ain't nothing but a thang, babe."
"Naw, I'm about to go, I have work in the morning." Tye's sister and brother left. Now it was just me, Tye, her mom, and daughter. Mike was sitting in the chair asleep until Tommy woke him up.
"Aye man we out, come lock your door." It took him a while to get him up. He locks the door and comes into the kitchen where I was talking to Tye while she was washing dishes.
"Kya come here, let me holla at you."
"Go ahead, I can hear you."
"Naw, this is private. I got something for you," and he goes into the bathroom. I just kept standing there talking to Tye as he was sitting on the toilet still fully dressed just staring at me.
"Kya, come here." I shook my head no. He got up and grabbed my arm, pulled me into the bathroom and closed the door.
"Stop playing Mike," and I tried to open the door. "Tye come get your cousin."

"No, get in here and sit down." I heard her mother say. Then the music stopped so it was very quiet.

"Why are you acting like that," he asked me. He was sitting on the toilet again trying to pull me on his lap. "Because this ain't cool, you know I gotta dude."

"Then why you come back?"

"I just came to kick it with you and my girl on your birthday. If I gave you the wrong impression, I apologize and now I'm about to go." I opened the bathroom door; my heart was beating a mile a minute because I didn't know what he was about to do to me. I had all types of crazy thoughts running through my head. I walked past Tye and her mom and rolled my eyes.

"I'll holla at you." I never looked her way. I was pissed because that was fucked up. Tye always let her mom run her life, she was the one that invited me over, she was supposed to be my Dogg and always have my back. I got out on the porch and Mike was behind me to lock the door, but when I got to the door the key wasn't in it so I couldn't leave.

"Mike, can you open the door?" He felt in his pockets.

"I can't find the key", and he started laughing and staggering across the porch. "Here it is. It's in my pocket. Come get it."

"Mike, would you stop playing?"

"I'm not playing I can't get 'em." I go to get the keys from his pocket and it's about twenty keys on the ring and it was dark on the porch. I'm looking through them trying to figure out which key it was and when I glance up in Mike's direction, he had his shirt off and was unbuckling his pants and they fell to his ankles. "What the hell are you doing?"

"I'm hot, and I'm ready to go to sleep." His words were slurring together. I knew he was drunk, so I tried to help him get his clothes back on. He grabbed my hand and rubbed it up against his manhood and it was hard as a brick. I snatched my hand back and he fell up against the wall. I felt sorry for him and didn't want his people seeing him like this. I got his pants back up just as they walked out on the porch.

"Could ya'll help me?"

"What is he doing?"
"Tryna strip." They were laughing so hard they couldn't hold him up. We finally got his shirt back on and got him back in the house. I handed Tye the keys.
"Can you find the right key to open the door?" She looked at the keys.
"That key is not even on this ring." She goes in the house and gets the key. I'm on the porch getting his drinks and stuff when I see his necklace and it's a fat rope with a big "M" on it. It must have come off when he took off his shirt. I went back into the house to give it to him, and he was lying on the couch.
"Aye Mike are you missing something?" and I held up his necklace. "It was on the porch." He opened one eye to see what I had.
"Keep it, so I'll know where it's at." I put it over my head and around my neck with pride because I had never had anything like this. This chain was like the one's Run DMC wore in their videos and it looked good around my neck. I left, Tye locked up his house and I went home and called Otis. It was only about 11:30pm so I didn't feel so bad about calling his parents house so late. I apologized to him because I saw what he was talking about, I knew I was wrong, and he meant well. He accepted my apology as usual, and he promised he'd be over Saturday afternoon after practice and that's what he did.

CHAPTER- 3

Monday morning, I got up bright and early so that I could make sure I was extra fly because I still had Mike's necklace and of course I was going to rock it. I put on a black and white schoolgirl pleaded mini skirt, a white turtleneck, and a black cashmere sweater so that the necklace would stand out. I wore my hair up in one big ponytail to the side with a long skinny braid on the left side full of black and white beads that lay over my shoulder. I didn't get to school at my regular early time because I wanted to be "casually late" I figured I could make my money between 0 period and homeroom that gave me a good 20 minutes. I walked in the classroom just as the bell was ringing; the teacher wasn't in yet, so I went over to Tye's table to see what was up with her.
"What's up girl?" I asked.
"Whazz up?"
"Shit, chillin' chillin'."
"So did you have fun Friday night at Mike's party?"
"Hell yeah, man I was fucked up."
"Me too, oh I see you still got Mike's necklace."
"Yeah, I haven't seen him. I was with my Boo all weekend."
"What did he say about you wearing that necklace?"
"He said that I had to give it back. I tried calling him all weekend, but he wasn't at home, and I paged him, but he didn't call me back."
"You gave him your number?"
"He already had it because he called me one day last week and he's cool, I don't mind if he calls me."

"Um, well he was with his girl Angelica all weekend that's probably why he didn't call you back," and she glanced at me out of the corner of her eye. I shrugged my shoulders. "That's nice." Then the teacher walked in the class. "Sorry I'm late. Everyone get your assignments out and let's get started." I went to my seat and did just that. After class Tye didn't wait for me like she usually did, she left with her other girl London, the girl that had slept with Mike a few months earlier. I didn't care I just hooked up with my other girls and went on what we called the block, which was the bricks on the floor right when you walked into the front door and made some money. I got compliments on this necklace all day, a lot of the guys were hating saying it was fake, but it didn't bother me because they were just mad. Tye didn't say too much to me all day. I saw her in the hallway going to third period and I ran to catch up with her.

"Tye what's up?"
"Nothing."
"What's wrong with you?"
"What you mean?"
"You've been acting funny all day."
"I'm just tired, the baby kept me up last night."
"Oh alright, well call me later I'm about to go home." I knew she had an attitude, but I didn't understand why.

    I went to work and put in four hours. When I got off, I went over Mike's to give him back his necklace, but he wasn't home. I knew Otis was coming over that night because we were going to the movies to see 'The Little Rascals' and I didn't want him mad at me, so I took it off and put it up. Mike would get his necklace another day. Otis and I went to the movies and when I came home, I had

a message on my answering machine. I pushed the play button it was Mike. "What's up Kya? My bad for not calling you right back I was in the middle of something, hit me on my hip when you get in so I can come get my necklace." Mike didn't know where I lived and I kind of didn't want him to. I sat down on the bed and returned his call.
 "Aye, I was getting ready to go out so I can drop it off."
 "Naw, I'm over my dudes not to far from you. Can I swoop by and pick it up?" Mike knew the area that I stayed in, but not the exact location. "And I'm not going home for a minute because I got a lot of running to do."
 "Alright." I gave him my address.
 "It's going to be a minute before I come."
 "Alright." I asked Otis if he would stay until Mike left and he did.

    I knew a minute to Mike meant an hour or so, so that gave Otis and me plenty of time to spend together. We lied on the couch and watched a couple of sitcoms. I was lying on his chest, and he had his arm around my shoulder and every now and then he would kiss me on my forehead. He always made me feel so good and that really turned me on. We had our intimate moment for what seemed like forever until I heard a car sitting in front of my house with the engine running. Mike also had a black T-Top Camero with an extended muffler, so you heard him coming. I got up and looked outside and it was him. He knocked on the door and I stepped out on the porch.
 "Oh, I see you were busy", he said.
 "What you mean?" He looked down at my pants and smiled. I looked down too and my zipper was down. I guess my face expressions made him laugh and I started

laughing too as I zipped my pants up. He looked over at Otis's car, which was a brand-new Altima that was parked in my driveway.
"Who's a cop?"
"My father-in-law."
"Your dad?"
"No, my dude's dad." He waved his hand and smacked his lips.
"Whatever, man I'll holla at you later." I gave him his necklace, he left, and I went back in the house with Otis.
"Is everything alright?"
"Yeah, why?"
"Because I have to get ready to go."
"Okay. Thanks for staying." I walked Otis to the side door so he would be closer to his car; I gave him a big hug and a kiss with a whole lot of tongue. "I love you baby."
"I love you too," and he went home.

****

Mike started calling me on the regular just to see how I was doing, or how my day went. I didn't have a problem with him calling because I talked to a couple of guys on the phone. I trusted myself and didn't think that anyone or anything could come between Otis and me because I wanted to marry this man and start a family. Mike would try to take me out, but I always told him no. He paid a lot of attention to what I was interested in because he always tried to take me to places that I wanted to go.

The middle of the week Mike was to leave and go to Vegas, he asked me if I wanted to go too but I couldn't miss school or work; otherwise, I would have gone. I hadn't seen too much of Mike since his party except every now and than over Tye's house because he had gotten custody of one of his daughters, Michelle. She was nine months, and he was busy caring for her, and I thought that was the sexiest thing ever for a man to take over the responsibilities of a child, especially with his busy life. Mike left for Vegas and Angelica stayed back to take care of his daughter and Tye made sure I was aware of this.

  Tye wanted to go and spend the day with Eric; he didn't go to school, so he was always at home. I got out of school at 10:45 am because I was in the work/study program and I had all my credits when I was in the eleventh grade, but they wouldn't let me graduate early. My fourth period class was a study hall and I refused to go to a study hall and then go home so I left after my third period class.
"Kya, when you leave today can I get a ride over Eric's?"
"I have to go home first and change my clothes and eat lunch." Eric's house was on the way to my job, if I went that way and I didn't mind.
"Okay, I'll just come over your house until you're ready."
"Meet me at my locker after third period." We get to my house and while I was in my room changing clothes, the phone rang.
"Hello?" It was Mike, he usually called me on my lunch, but I didn't think he would be calling me from Vegas.
"What's up girl?"
"Hey, how are you doing?"
"Alright. Man, I met a bunch of celebrities up here. I'm staying in the Lady Luck Hotel and this place is nice. So, what's going on down there?"
"Nothing, the same ole', same ole'."
"Hey, Kya" Tye interrupted. "Can I get some of

these barbeque chips on top of the refrigerator?"
"I don't care."
"Who is that?" Mike asked.
"That's your crazy cousin, Tye."
"Oh, tell her I said what's up?"
"Tye, Mike said what's up?"
"That's him on the phone?"
"Um hum."
"Tell him I said hello." Mike and I talked for another five to ten minutes while I finished getting dressed. I got off the phone and went into the kitchen to make my lunch. I fixed my plate, put it in the microwave on sensor and sat down at the table with Tye, who was eating her chips.
"So, what are you and Eric going to do today?"
"Probably nothing," she said with a disgusted look on her face. "Is Mike still in Vegas?"
"Yeah, he said he'd be back this weekend."
"What did he call you for?"
"Just to see how I was doing and to say what's up."
"Um." I finished eating my lunch and dropped Tye off over Eric's house. We didn't say two words the whole ride there. We pulled in front of Eric's house, Tye opened the car door.
"Thanks", she said as she was getting out then she slammed my door shut. I just shook my head and went on to work thinking in my head, *this girl got issues*.

  The next day at school I didn't say anything to Tye because I wasn't about to kiss her ass. I didn't know what her problem was and at this point I didn't care. After zero period, I was talking to my cousin and Shawn, as we were about to go down the steps when I saw Tye standing in the stairway. "Hey Kya" I turned in her direction.

"What's up?"
"Girl, let me tell you about yesterday. Man, Eric is a trip" and she proceeded to tell me about her day with Eric the day before. By the time we got to the first floor she had told me everything, all the gory details and it sounded like she had a good time.
"Aye, watch this." I looked over at her and she had a bottle of mace in her hand.
"Man, what are you doing?" I asked.
"Close your eyes and walk fast." She sprayed the mace into the crowd behind us. Tye had a lot of enemies and a few of theme were behind us. We heard a lot of moans and groans, but we never looked back. We went and stood against the lockers outside of our classrooms because her class was right across from mine and did our normal everyday flirting.
"Aye, Kya."
"I'm leaving after third period. Can I get a rid to the crib?"
"Why certainly. Meet me at my locker." Tye was standing at my locker at 10:45. I grabbed my books and jacket, and we went outside and got into the car.
"Oh, can you stop by Mike's first? I need to get something."
"Mike's not back yet."
"I know." I didn't say anything else. When we pulled in front of Mike's house she got out and knocked on the door. I'm looking closely because I'm curious to see who's going to open the door. A tall dark-skinned girl with real long, pretty, black hair opened the door wearing a purple and white silk pajama shirt and a pair of jogging pants. Tye went inside and closed the door. She returned in about two to three minutes laughing and smiling. She got back into the car.

"Who is that?" I asked.
"That's Angelica, Mike's girlfriend." Then again, she looked at me out of the corner of her eye, but I showed no expression. "Oh, I didn't tell you she was staying here now?"
"You probably did." I said nonchalantly. I was jealous as hell, but I wasn't about to let her know that. That's when I realized that I was really into Mike.

****

Otis had gotten a part time job at Friendly's, a hamburger and ice cream place, so we didn't see each other as much anymore, although we tried every moment we could. This particular day Otis was at work and, my phone rang.
"Hey, Kya."
"What's up Mike?" and a big smile came across my face.
"When did you get back?"
"Late last night, I was going to call you, but I figured you were asleep. So, what you are doing today?"
"I don't know I'm getting dressed now."
"Well, why don't you come by when you get done? I got something for you."
"Alright, I'll see you in a bit" and we hung up; just as I was sitting on the bed putting lotion on my body the phone rang again.
"What's up girl?"
"Shit, getting dressed."
"What you about to do?"
"Nothing. Why, what's up?"
"Well why don't you come over so we can start on this video?" Tye and I were partners on this report we had to

do for school on child abuse and we were going to make a video for our display.
"Okay, give me like an hour."
"Alright" and I hung up. I got dressed. I put on a jogging suit and a starter pull over because it was still kind of cold out for April. I arrived at Mike's house, and I was knocking at the door for a long time. The inside door on the porch was opened so I knew he was in there. He came to the door; his eyes were red, and he was walking very slowly.
"Dang, it took you long enough."
"I fell asleep." He stretched and went back into the house. I locked the screen door and followed him in, he lay back down on the couch, and I sat at the other end by his feet. I sat there for a couple of minutes neither of us saying a word. I smacked him on his foot.
"I didn't come over here to watch you sleep."
"Man, I'm tired. I kicked it all while I was down there."
He tried to sit up and his foot hit the table, which drew my eyes in that direction. I saw a whole lot of gold rings and a few necklaces lying on the table. It was this one ring that had a dollar sign on it that really caught my eye. I picked it up and was admiring it.
"You like that?"
"Yeah, this is pretty slick." I set it back down on the table. He got up and knelt between my legs.
"What are you doing?" and he smiled at me. "I know this is not what you're talking about you brought back for me."
"Oh, naw." He got up, looked on top of his big screen TV, got a CD and put it into the CD player.
"Listen to this." It was the new R-Kelly remix of 'Your Bodies Calling' and it was not yet down here, and he knew I was really into music.

"Oh, that's nice, that's for me?"
"You like that?" He came and knelt back down between my legs and looked into my eyes. "You are so pretty."
"Thank you" and I kind of smirked. The next thing I knew he was pulling down my jogging pants. "Oh, you are trippin'." He didn't say anything he just proceeded to take them down. I was sitting slouched down with my head on the back of the couch and my butt almost on the edge. Mike grabbed both of my legs and put them over my shoulders. I don't know when he took his manhood out, but before I could say stop, he was sticking it in. I reached my arms around my legs to push his chest.
"Mike, get up, this ain't cool." He started moaning, and then he pulled it out and came on my stomach and in his hand. I was mad, but at the same time I wasn't. I didn't want it, but it wasn't that bad, this brother was really packing. "You bet not have cum in me."
"I didn't", he said breathing hard. I had stopped taking my birth control pills because Otis and I wanted a baby, and I didn't want any problems. I got up and fixed my clothes. I was very distraught. I guess the look on my face told it all.
"What's wrong with you?" I turned my lips to the side and shook my head.
"Nothing."
"Then why you look like you just lost your best friend?"
"I wasn't ready for this to happen." I already knew that if I had sex with someone, I always put my heart into it, I was already falling for Mike, and this would just make matters worse.
"I saw you admiring that ring over there; let me see how it looks on you." I put it on my index finger of my right hand.

"Yeah, that looks good on you" and it sure did. "You can have it." That whole distraught feeling died instantly. I started smiling, and so did he.
"Thank you," I said. "Well, I have to go. I'm supposed to go over Tye's so we can get started on our school assignment.
"Okay baby, I'll talk to you later," and he kissed me on the cheek. I went home, washed up and got myself together. I went over Tye's; we wrote out our report, but she didn't have the camcorder, so we didn't get to video tape it. I left her house, went back home, laid down to sort my thoughts and I fell asleep.

CHAPTER- 4

Senior prom was two weeks from now and Otis and I both were working hard to get our money right because we had two proms to attend his and mine. I knew I had to be extra fly for mine because I had gone out for prom queen. I bought a long black fitted dress with a split that came all the way up to my mid-thigh on the right side with black pumps, sheer black panty hose and black gloves that came to my elbow since my dress was strapless. Everything was going well that following week, my mom had bought me a brand-new car, that only had 38 miles on it when she gave it to me. It was a green Sundance with 4-doors and a tape cassette, it was nice. All I needed now was some tint on the windows, some rims and some beats to set it off right.

     That next week came like tomorrow, and I still had so much to do. It was a good thing that our senior picnic was the same day because that meant we didn't have school and I didn't have to go to work, so I had all day to get ready and I needed it. Tye and I went down to the picnic for like an hour, but it was boring, so we left. I had a hair appointment at 1:00 pm so we went to my house and chilled for a while. I dropped Tye off about 12:15 and headed toward the salon because I didn't really know where I was going, and I wanted to pick out a hair style because my mom was letting me finally get a perm and get my hair cut. I found a parking spot by some nice cars because I didn't want to park my new whip by any "hoopties", and went inside and signed in. She called me back right away, even though I was fifteen minutes early and got started. I grabbed a couple of books and looked

through them while she gave me a relaxer. I found a real nice style, it was short on the left side, but it was feathered, the top was short too, but not as short as the left side and it got shorter as it went down to the right, it was feathered also, and the back was still long. She finished relaxing, deep conditioning and blow-drying my hair and she started to cut it. She had the chair turned away from the mirror so I couldn't see what she was doing. When I looked down on the floor and saw all my hair I started crying.
"What's wrong, you don't like it?" she asked. I just shrugged my shoulders as tears streamed down my face. "Just wait until it's done it'll be real pretty, I promise." I sat there for the next hour in silence. She kept asking me questions about school and prom, but I really wasn't in the mood, and I think it showed because after awhile she didn't say anything else. When she got done, she handed me a small mirror and turned the chair halfway around. "Are your ready?" I looked up and she had a big smile on her face.
"I guess." She turned the chair the rest of the way around, so I was facing the mirror. She had hooked me up. I didn't say anything I was just checking it out at all angles. She was looking at me with a worried look on her face. I just kept looking at my hair. I finally smiled at her, winked, gave her a thumbs up and shook my head yes all at the same time. "So how do I get it back like this?" She told me how to style it and which type of comb to use. I paid her and went outside to get in my car. I cracked both front windows, put Ant Banks in the cassette player, adjusted the bass and blasted my music all the way to the nail shop.

    It was well after 4 pm and Otis said he'd be to get me about 6, he was always prompt and I still had a lot to

do. I went to get my nails done ran over Mike's because he wanted to see my new hairstyle. He didn't know that I had gotten a new car. I pulled up in his driveway blasting my factory radio. I got out and knock on the door. He came to the door quickly, closed the house door and came out on the porch. "Whose car you got?"
"Mine." I said with a smile.
"When you get that?"
"About two weeks ago. It's my graduation gift from my mom because I didn't have any babies while I was in high school."
"Oh, that's nice."
"Can I come in?"
"Um, I'm in the middle of something right now." I smacked my lips.
"Oh, well do you like my hair?"
"Awe you look so cutie, here" he handed me twenty dollars.
"What's this for?"
"When you get crowned for prom queen take some pictures for me." He kissed my on my cheek and sent me on my way. It was almost 5:30 now so I sped home. I got there in about seven minutes, and I went into the bathroom to freshen up. I was fully dressed by 5:55. My mom was helping me with my make up when we heard Otis knock on the door. My mom ran and got her camera before she let him in and started snapping pictures as he walked in the door. I came out of the bathroom and walked into the living room. Otis put my corsage he brought me on my wrist. We took some pictures then we walked out to get into his dad's Maxima. We were rolling in style. We stopped by my dad's, grandparents, his house, his aunts, cousins, and then we had to go get Tye because neither she

nor her boyfriend had cars. We got there a little late, but nothing had started jumping. We ate and danced then it was time to crown the queen. I didn't make it for queen, but I was first attendant because the girl that beat me was a cheerleader and she only beat me by two votes, so I was still crowned, I received a bouquet of flowers and a big trophy. Otis and I took a picture, and I took one by myself. We danced and mingled a little bit longer than we left because we had to take Tye back home and we had reservations out in Montrose, which was twenty minutes away. We ate dinner at a real nice restaurant and then we went to the room he had gotten for us. For some reason I had an attitude with Otis, but I didn't know why. We go into the Motel room, and I felt totally uncomfortable. The lock on the door was loose like someone had kicked the door in. The bedding looked like it was from the 1950's; there were little holes in the spread and the carpet looked dirty. I didn't say anything because I knew he was trying. I took off my clothes and put everything on the table, even my shoes. I threw the comforter on the floor and pulled the sheets all the way back to make sure they were clean. We got in the bed and instead of Otis making love to me like he always did; he fucked the shit out of me. With each hard stroke he told me he loved me. I started crying silently because I know that he was a good man, and I was doing him wrong. When we got done, we were lying in the bed holding each other when I saw a roach crawling on the wall. I followed it around with my eyes for about 20 minutes until I lost sight of it. Otis was asleep, and I had to go to the bathroom, but I was scared to get up. Now, I'm lying here emotionally distraught and afraid of this damn roach, so I started crying again. "Otis", I shook his shoulder.

"Hum."
"I want to go home."
"What's wrong?" he turned to face me.
"I don't feel comfortable here."
"I paid all this money for this room, man."
"I'm sorry, but I want to go home." We got up to get dressed; I shook out every piece of my clothing before I put them on, and I tapped the heel of my shoes to make sure there wasn't anything in them. We went back to my house and my mom let Otis stay the night because she didn't want him driving out this late. The next morning and went to Cedar Point. I didn't really enjoy myself because I had Mike on my mind the whole day.

    The next weekend was his prom, he went to a pretty much all white school, so we did the bunny hop all night and listen to music I had never heard before. The only song that I knew was the YMCA and that's because they play it in a lot of movies. We went back to his house to change our clothes and to get a little quickie. Then we had to go back to his school for a lock-in. We had to stay there all night otherwise they would call our parents and since Otis's parents were volunteers, there was no escaping. We took a whole lot of pictures, and I took a couple that I knew I was going to give to Mike. We left his school around 6:30 am the next morning and I went home and slept for most of the day.

CHAPTER- 5

My graduation was this coming Wednesday, and we only got six free tickets each and I made sure that my parents, grandparents and Otis got a ticket before anybody else. Otis sat with my mom since he came by himself. When they called my name, the audience went wild like I was a celebrity. When I got to the end of the stage to walk down the steps Mike was standing there with his camera, he started taking pictures of me and it kind of startled me because I didn't expect him to be there. He must have been there with Tye. I was distracted and wasn't paying attention to what I was doing, and the banister went under my sleeve, and I kept walking until it snatched me back, luckily, I was walking slowly, otherwise I would have gotten jacked up. "Congratulations baby!"
"Thank you" and I walked back to my seat. After graduation was over Otis and my parents were waiting for me in the lobby. I kissed my grandparents, and my dad and Otis handed me a half dozen of roses I and gave him a hug. "Thank you, baby,", I said showing all my teeth then I grabbed his hand.
"What do ya'll want to do?" My mom asked.
"Well, I'm hungry." I knew that my dad really didn't like eating out and my mom had to go to work in a couple of hours. "Otis and I can go tonight, and we can go as a family on Friday because it's getting late."
"Are you sure Kya?"
"Yeah, I'll see you later." Otis and I left. When we got outside Mike was sitting across from where we had parked with his music beating in his truck.
"Hey Kya" I looked in his direction. "Come take a picture with me." I looked at Otis and he shrugged his shoulders

like whatever. I walked over to his truck, and he had Eric take a couple of pictures of us.
"Oh, you got jokes", I said in a low tone so that Otis couldn't hear me.
"What?" he asked and started laughing. I walked back over to where Otis was standing, put my arms around his waist, he put his arm around my shoulder, and we walked over to his car. He opened the door for me, and we went to Applebee's to get some steak. He took me home so that I could change into some shorts and get out of those itchy panty hose. We went to get his cousin James and a couple of his other boys, and we all went over Eric's house because his mom was never home. We had a couple of drinks and just chilled until like 1 or 2 in the morning. Otis took me home, walked me to the door and gave me a real good night kiss. "I love you."
"I love you too. Call me when you wake up in the morning."
"I'll call you when I get home tonight." I smiled and he kissed me again. I went inside, took a hot shower and got ready for bed. Mike had left a message on my answering machine to call him when I got in, but I didn't bother because I was waiting for my Boo to call.

****

I had taken the rest of the week off work so that I could enjoy sleeping in because they were talking about hiring me in full time, which meant that I had to get up at 6:30 am and I had been doing that since school was out and I needed a break. Mike called me at 7:00 am and I answered the phone in a sleepy voice. "Hello?"
"Good morning."
"Hey."

"You not going to work today?"
"No, I'm off."
"Why didn't you call me when you got home last night?"
"It was late."
"Oh, well what you are doing next Saturday?"
"I don't know why?"
"Because I want you to go to Cedar Point with me."
"Oh really?"
"Can you do that?"
"I'll see what I can do."
"Alright call me when you get up."

****

  I woke up bright and early for a Saturday morning because my little brother Antwon and I had a Dentist appointment and Mike and I had plans to go to Cedar Point. I called Mike to make sure our plans were still on, but he didn't answer so I watched cartoons until Antwon got ready. We went to our appointment, and it seemed like we were there forever. It was 10:13 when we left there, and our appointment was at 8:45. I felt my pager vibrating in my pocket. I looked at it and it was Mike. I went to a pay phone, looked in my ashtray and found a quarter and called him back.
"Are we still on for today?"
"Yeah, but I got to make some runs so give me like an hour."
"Alright."
 Antwon and I went to get some breakfast and headed home. Mike got to my house around 12:15, it took two hours to get to Cedar Point and I was trying to hurry up and get away before my mom came home from work or

Antwon saw who picked me up. I was sitting in the living room watching BET patiently waiting for him to arrive. I had the front door open so that I could see him pull up. Antwon was down the basement, I knew he wouldn't tell on me, but I didn't want him to feel like he had to lie if he was asked. I heard Mike's Camero pull around the corner. "Aye, I'm out." I yelled to Antwon, but he didn't say anything, so I assumed he was asleep. I turned the TV off, went out the front door and closed it behind me. When I got into the car Mike gave me a kiss on my cheek. I looked down at his gear and I kind of frowned because he always dressed nice, I mean everything brand name from head to toe. He looked at me looking at him.
"I'm not wearing this. I need to run to the store and buy something to wear and get some shoes." I didn't comment I just looked at him. We went to the west side to the plaza, and he told me to stay in the car. About five songs came on the radio including the commercials so now it's getting closer to 1 pm and I'm agitated because we were supposed to have left at 11 am because I had a 12 am curfew. He got dressed in the car and by 1 pm we were on the road. I fell asleep on the ride and when I woke up, we had about another 15 or 20 minutes to go before we arrived. We walked through the gate hand in hand like we were so in love, we rode all the new rides that I didn't get to ride with Otis first. "Are you hungry?"
"Yeah, a little." We went to a burger stand and I got a cheeseburger meal, he didn't want that, so we walked around until he found something he wanted. They were selling these big drumsticks like something off the Flintstones, I don't know what kind of bird that was, but he slammed it like it was the first thing he had eaten in weeks. I had the time of my life; I couldn't remember the last time

I had laughed so much. We had so much fun. Mike was very good at sports, so he won me three medium size animals, four big ones and three teamed basketballs. Otis had won me some things too, and I know it's the thought that counts, but I was into Mike, and I liked the one's he got me because they were not just bigger, but they were from him. We walked around the park all day, riding all the rides and eating. I had cotton candy, candy apples, funnel cakes, pizza, hamburgers and pretty much anything that I wanted. I know he had to have spent a good three hundred dollars that day and he wasn't pressed.

    We left the park about nine because we didn't want to get caught in the traffic. I was exhausted and so was he. I couldn't wait to get home and get in my bed. I had leaned the seat back and closed my eyes after awhile I felt the car stop and Mike was getting out. I looked around and we were at a hotel. The first thing that came to my mind was *I'm not about to fuck this dude, so I hope he don't waste his money.* He got back in the car and drove around back. I just looked at him.
"Come on", he said. I got out and slowly walked behind him just trying to think fast as to how I was going to get out of this. We go into the room, and he goes into the bathroom and turns on the water. I guess he thought that would drown out his conversation, but it didn't.
"Were you sleeping? Well, I was calling to check on you. I probably won't make it home tonight, it's a good night. Oh yeah. Okay, well I'll talk to you later." Then I heard the toilet flesh, he didn't even use the bathroom. When he came out of the bathroom, I acted like I was asleep in the chair. He pulls the spread back on the bed and lies down on top of the blanket.

"Kya, come lay down with me." I didn't move. "Kya?"
"Huh."
"Come lay down with me." I get up and sit on the bed with one leg on the bed and the other on the floor. He grabbed my arm and pulled me toward him and started kissing me very passionately in the mouth and I was enjoying it, so I kissed him back. He started unbuttoning my shorts, I moved his hands away, but he put them right back on my zipper and then started pulling my shorts down to my knees and pulled my shirt and bra up. He started sucking on my breast, it felt so good, but I didn't like it because it was cheating, and it was wrong.
"Mike."
"What's the matter baby?"
"I don't want to do this."
"What's wrong?" I just started crying. He held me then wiped my tears.
"Don't cry." I think he knew that I was in love with Otis, and he respected that at the time.
"Come on, let's go." I got up and fixed my clothes, he fixed the bed and went back to the office and told them that he had an emergency at home and had to leave. They refunded his money because we were only there like a half an hour, and we headed home. We didn't talk much on the way home because I acted like I was asleep. I got home about 12:15 am. We sat in the car and talked for a minute, he parked his car behind this big tree in front our house, so my mom couldn't see if she looked out of the window. Even though his windows were tinted, and his inside light was red, we didn't want to take any chances. He kissed me goodbye, and I went into the house. My mom was asleep, so I went into my room and closed the door. I got ready for bed and watched Apollo as I held my new teddy bears.

Monday morning couldn't come fast enough. I couldn't wait to show Tye the pictures Mike and I had taken at Cedar Point, since she was going around telling everybody that "*Mike didn't really like me and all he wanted to do was fuck.*" When I got to zero period Tye was already there because Antwon had overslept and wasn't going to make the bus, so he asked me could I wait for him and give him a ride. He wasn't allowed to drive the Horizon; I had given him to school because he didn't have a parking permit yet. I went and sat down at my table, and then Tye came over. "So did you and Mike have a good time a Cedar Point?"
"Who told you?"
"Mike."
"Hell yeah, I had fun. I got so many stuffed animals and stuff its ridicules and here look at our picture." I went in my purse and pulled it out.
"Awe, ain't that cute. Go show London, she's going to be pissed because he never took her nowhere or did nothing for her."
"Man, you are silly." Tye started talking louder.
"So, what ride was ya'll on?" she asked while looking at the picture.
"The Magnum."
"You look like you were scared as hell." My cousin Latoya comes over to our table.
"What ya'll looking at?"
"A picture of your cousin and Mike at Cedar Point." Then here comes London.
"Let me see." Tye shows her the picture.
"Oh, ya'll kickin' it now?"
"Naw, we just cool."

"What Otis say about ya'll been so cool?" I just kind of laughed under my breath and smirked.
"Let me worry about that one." Then the bell rang so everyone went to there assign seats. I was really expecting to get the cold shoulder from Tye all day, but to my surprise she was actually her normal self. We kicked it more this day than we had in a long time.

   All week Otis had really been acting shady. He hadn't spent any time with me and every time we talked, he acted real distant and every time I tried to spend time with him, he was busy. Tye and I were talking, and I mentioned the way Otis had been acting.
"Girl, I don't know what's up with Otis, but he's really been acting funny." She gave me that look out of the corner of her eye.
"For real?" I knew she had something to do with it, but I just couldn't put my finger on it. When Friday came and I hadn't seen Otis all week I went over his house. I knocked on the door and his brother let me in.
"Hello." I said to his mother who was sitting at the kitchen table watching television.
"Hello. How are you doing?"
"Good, how about yourself?"
"Tired, it's been a long week."
"I can imagine."
"Well Otis is back in the TV room; you can go back there." I took my shoes off and walked back to the TV room. Otis was lying on the couch watching TV; he looked up and saw it was me than rolled his eyes. My heart dropped to my stomach, and I felt nauseated because he had never acted this way towards me.
"What's wrong with you?"

"I really don't want to talk about it right now." I go over to the couch and kiss him on the lips like we always greeted each other, but he didn't kiss me back. I took a deep breath to try to relax my mind. I move his arm so he could sit up. I sat down on the couch and pulled him back down so his head was on my lap. We sat there for like five minutes in total silence.

"Otis, what's wrong baby? You know the fact that you're ignoring me, is killing me. Let me know what's on your mind." He sat up and looked me in the eyes. *Damn he is fine*. I thought.

"So where were you last weekend?"

"I told you I was going to Cedar Point with some friends."

"Some friends like Mike?"

"Yeah, he went, but baby it wasn't nothing, we were just having a good time." His eyes stared turning red. I knew he was pissed.

"If it was nothing than why didn't you tell me?"

"Because I wanted to go, but I knew that you wouldn't approve if you knew that Mike was going."

"So, you went behind my back."

"Otis, don't do this." He laughed under his breath and shook his head.

"I went down to Angelica's job this afternoon." My head turned so fast I thought I had gotten whiplash.

"What?"

"Yeah, we had a nice long talk, and she didn't know that Mike took you to Cedar Point either." I knew Tye was behind this because nobody else could have given Otis all this information about who Angelica was and where she worked. So, I just sat there dumbfounded. "So where is the picture ya'll took together?" Now I'm pissed at myself and really at Tye because she was supposed to be my dogg.

"I don't know" and I rolled my eyes and crossed my arms over my chest.
"So did you fuck him?" Otis never really used file language.
"Is that what you think of me?"
"I don't know what to think."
"Otis, I love you and to be honest, he tried, but I couldn't do that to you." By this time my eyes were full of tears because I knew that I had hurt him and those were not my intentions.
"Well, you really have a strange way of showing your love." I didn't say anything; I just sat there for the next half hour or so deep in thought. My pager had gone off two times, but I just hit the button because I wasn't in the mood.

It was starting to get late, and I wanted to be home before my mom went to work. We said our good-byes and he walked me to my car and just held me in his arms.
"Call me when you get home."
"I will baby." I got into my car and bagged out of the driveway. When I got to the stop sign, I looked at my pager and it read 111, that was Mike's code, then I pushed the button to go to the next page, and it read 111-411, that was Mike again. I wasn't about to stop at a pay phone because Otis knew about how long it took me to get home and I didn't want Mike to ask me to come over. I got on the highway and mashed it all the way home. I got home in eleven minutes from the west side and that's because I got caught by a red light. My mom was still asleep, so I went into my room and closed the door so that I could call Otis. We talked for about a half an hour, he said he forgave me, but I know he was mad at me. We got off the phone

because he said he was going over his cousin James house to chill. I hung up and called Mike.
"Hello." He answered the phone on the second ring.
"What's up?"
"Man, where your little punk ass boyfriend at?"
"Why, what's wrong with you?" I already knew I just wanted to hear his side of the story.
"Why that motha fucka go down to Angelica's job bothering her with some bull shit?"
"What are you talking about?"
"He told her I took you to Cedar Point and we took pictures together and everything else."
"Oh, well how you think he found out about that?"
"You."
"Come on man, I'm not trying to fuck up my shit. You need to check your cousin because her big mouth had to be the one to give him all the information. I don't even know where that girl work at. Well, what did she say?"
"She told him not to come bothering her at her job with that and now she around here talking crazy."
"Well, you should have thought about that before you asked me to go, you can't be mad at nobody but yourself."
"Naw, he gon' pay. Don't let me see that motha fucka."
"Whatever, I'm about to go cause you on some bull shit."
"Oh, we'll see." I just hung up the phone.

CHAPTER- 6

My mom had planed a family trip to Alabama. Otis and I weren't really on the best of terms because he didn't trust me and I had kind of pushed away, but we were trying to work out our differences. He was doing everything in his power to try to make me love him all over again.

He took me everywhere he went, but I had gotten so use to the finer things that Mike was giving me and I was infatuated with all the things his money was bringing me, that I ignored all the good things that Otis was doing for me. I didn't realize that this was real love that I had right in my face. Mike and I were doing everything that couples do like going to the movies, to dinner, he'd give me money for shoes and outfits, he'd get my hair done and we were having sex. But he was not my man, not really.

Otis had called me the day we were leaving for our vacation.
"Hey, Kya, what are you doing today?"
"Well, I have to get my stuff together so we can get ready to leave and then I have a few runs to make. Why, what's up?"
"I wanted to spend some time with you before you left."
"What time is it? Um 11:30, alright give me to about 3 and I should be done with everything."
"Alright, I'll see you later." We hung up the phone and I called Mike, he wasn't home, so I paged him because he was supposed to give me fifty dollars so that I could have some spending money while I was out of town. I had pulled out of the street game because Mike was taking good care of me. I had gotten hired in full time at my job and I had gotten a raise. The only bill I had was my house phone

and it was only forty dollars a month. While I was waiting for Mike to return my call, I called this guy Mark that I had meet a couple of weeks ago, we were just friends because he was married, and his wife was pregnant. He was like fifteen years older than me, but he was going to give me fifty dollars too and he didn't answer his phone either, so I left him a message. "Aye this Kya, I'm probably going to be leaving about four so I'm going to need to see you before 3:30". I figured that would give me enough time before Otis got there. Otis arrived at 2:59 and Mike nor Mark had returned my call, the banks were closed and all I had was sixty dollars in my pocket and I planned on shopping while I was down there, and this was not enough. We watched videos then we went outside to sit on the porch and the phone rang.
"What up girl?" It was Mark.
"Nothing, it took you long enough." I took the phone and went into the house.
"I was at the hospital with my wife."
"Is she alright?"
"Yeah, she's having a little complication with the baby, but I don't want to talk about that right now. So do you want me to bring you that money?"
"No, I'll meet you at the Reservoir in about fifteen minutes."
"Alright." I went back outside with Otis for another five minutes because the park was only a five-minute walk from my house.
"Aye, let's go to the park and play some one on one."
"You don't want to get beat before you leave."
"What's up?"
"Go get the ball." I ran down the basement and got the basketball and we walked to the park. We played for a

while I had made two baskets to his one and it was his ball and I saw Mark pull his van into the parking lot.
"Hold on Otis, I got to go to the bathroom. I'll be right back. Get you some practice." I ran to the back of the building and walked around to the side where Mark could see me. We sat on the wall and talked for a minute and then he handed me the money. I gave him a hug and a kiss on the cheek.
"Thank you."
"Well, I have to go because I have to go pick up my son from his grandmother's."
"Okay, then, I'll call you when I came back."
"Walk me to my car." I didn't want to because I know if I came from behind the building Otis would see me. When I looked his way, he had his back turned and Mark's car wasn't far so I figured he wouldn't see me. When we got to Mark's van I look, and Otis's back was still turned.
"Give me another hug", Mark said. I gave him a quick friendly hug and when I turned around Otis was staring right at me. "Well let me go before your little boyfriend gets mad" and he started laughing. I slowly walked back to the basketball court.
"You get your practice in?"
"Yeah, let me beat you right quick so we can get this over with."
"What's wrong with you?"
"Nothing." We played to ten, he beat me by one point, but I represented. We walked back to my house.
"Dang, you didn't have to throw that up in my face."
"What are you talking about now?"
"Who was that guy?"
"He's just a friend."

"Oh, I don't have friends that give me money." I don't know how he knew that he had given me any money, but I wasn't even about to go there with him.
"Well believe me if it was something serious, I wouldn't have brought you with me. He didn't say anything we just kept walking. When we got to my house he was sitting on the porch, and I was on the sidewalk bouncing the ball when the phone rang again.
"What's up Kya?" It was Mike.
"Hey you." I throw the ball to Otis and put up one finger signaling that I'd be back in a minute.
"So, what are you doing?"
"Nothing, just sitting on the porch."
"Are you coming to get this change?"
"Can't you bring it to me?" I knew Mike wouldn't act up over my house with my mom home.
"No, I'm in the middle of something," which meant he didn't want me to stay.
"Alright give me like fifteen or twenty minutes."
"Okay, try to hurry up." I go back outside with Otis and he's looking like he has an attitude. I kissed him on the lips and sat down on the second step between his legs.
"Don't be mad at me but I have to go somewhere real quick and it'll only take fifteen minutes, you can stay here with my brother, or you can go get us some ice cream and by the time you get back I'll be back."
"Where you gotta go." I didn't want to lie because we were being open with each other.
"Over Mike's." He rolled his eyes.
"I don't want to stay here, and I don't want any ice cream."
"Okay then I'll call you when I get back."

"See there you go brushing me off again, I'm tired of being put second. This is supposed to be our time." I sighed and put my hands over my face.
"Well, what do you want me to do?"
"I can take you; you say you'll are just friends, and you don't have anything to hide."
"Okay, let's go just don't pull in his driveway." On the ride over there I knew that I was making a mistake, but I didn't know how to get out of it I wanted to spend time with Otis, and I needed this money, besides Mike wasn't my man. What could he say? When we got to Mike's Street, I had Otis stop two houses down. It was dark and a lot of cars were on the street, I figured he wouldn't know the difference. I ran up the street and rang Mike's doorbell, he came to the door after I started knocking. He let me onto the porch and closed the door.
"I don't have any change", and he handed me three twenties. I had a ten, but I wasn't giving it to him.
"Thank you", and I gave him a hug and a kiss on the lips, and he stuck his tongue in my mouth.
"You are so nasty" and I pushed him away. He looked out of the window.
"How did you get here?"
"My homey. Why?"
"Oh, I just asked."
"Alright, let me get home and finish packing."
"Alright, call me when you get back and have fun."
"Thank you and I'll call you." When he let me out the door, I saw him looking around, I guess he was trying to see which car I was in. I slowly walked to the car hoping he'd be in the house by the time I got to Otis's car, but when I turned around, he was still watching. I got in the car, by the time Otis turned his car around I looked through the side

window to see if Mike was still watching, but he wasn't he had come outside and was getting into his car. We turned the corner before he got all the way in his car and turned around, but we were caught by a red light. Mike flew up behind us, slammed on his breaks and was about to get out, but the light turned, and we pulled off. He followed us all the way to the Heights on Otis's bumper, so when we got close enough for me to walk home, I told Otis to let me out. "He must want me for something, I can walk home." He stopped in the middle of the street, the car was still rolling when I opened the door, by the time the car came to a complete stop I was already out of the car. Mike put his car in park and opened his door and Otis pulled off. I was standing in the street in front of Mike's car so he couldn't go anywhere.
"What the fuck are you doing?"
"Why the fuck you bring that nigga to my house?"
"Man, you on some bull shit. It's not like he don't know where you stay." He didn't say anything else, he just got into his car, put it in drive and mashed on the gas. I jumped out of the way and landed in the grass. When I looked up both Mike and Otis were out of site. I walked home pissed at myself for being so stupid. I should have handled this differently.

I got home and was sitting on the porch when my mom came to the door.
"Where's Otis?"
"He left."
"Oh, well are you ready?" I shook my head yes, then the phone rang. I answered in on the firsts ring.
"Hello?"
"Hello", it was Otis.

"Where are you?"
"At home."
"How you get home so fast?"
"I went down the back streets and got on the expressway down there by East High School."
"I am so sorry, if I would have known he was going to be like that I would have gone on my own."
"Don't worry about it. Are you okay?"
"Yeah, he didn't do anything to me." Then my line beeped.
"Okay, well let me go in here and finish getting ready" and the line beeped again.
"Alright call me when you get back."
"I will baby, I love you."
"I love you too." I hung up the phone and it rang right back. I just let the answering machine pick it up because I assumed it was Mike. By the time I got to my room I heard my answering machine. *'I ain't mad at you'* by Tupac was playing in the background.
"*Hey, what up, I'm sorry I missed your call, but if you leave me a name, number, and a message, then I'll get back to you as soon as possible, but if you don't, I won't be mad at you*" and I said that part like Tupac said on his song.
"Aye, I was calling to see if you made it home okay and I wanted to tell you that I'm sorry. I'll talk to you later."
When the phone beeped, I pressed the delete button and got my bags and put them in the car.

CHAPTER- 7

It took fourteen hours to drive to Alabama and we stayed with my Aunt Loren, who was bed written and by the second day I was ready to go home. The days were fun, but the nights were long because they had big water bugs and roaches. It was eight of us staying in a two-bedroom apartment. My mom and her boyfriend ended up sleeping outside in the van, which wasn't fair because my mom knew I was terrified of bugs. Her house wasn't nasty, but she stayed in an apartment complex and her neighbor had four kids and they were trifling, so all their bugs came next door. I didn't want to hurt anybody's feelings or make anyone think that I thought I was better than them, so I tried to stay outside and away from the bugs.
"Aye, let's go sit outside on the porch." My cousin Wilma and I sat outside until it got dark and just chilled, but she was too girly for me. I needed some excitement in my life. That night Wilma and I cleaned the whole house from top to bottom. We sprayed so much roach spray and put down so much roach powder we had to close my aunt in her room and opened all the windows in the house and we went outside for about an hour or so. I got a good night sleep that night.

When I woke up that next morning, I got my clothes out of the van and got dressed. My little cousin Tray, he was fifteen, but he was the coolest, we use to hang tight when he lived in Akron. He was in the streets gang banging, so his mom figured that moving him away would be a good move for him. He was sitting in the living room putting on his shoes.
"What you about to do?"

"Go to the store."
"Hold on I'm rollin' with you." I put on my tennis shoes, and we left. We walked to the store about seven blocks and there were five guys standing outside the store. One of the guys stood out from the rest of them, he was a cutie.
Before I walked into the store, I looked back to get one last peek and he was looking my way and our eyes caught. I smiled and went into the store. I brought some Funyun's, a Pepsi and a pack of big red. When I walked out, they were still standing there.
"Tray, did you want me to get you something?"
"Naw, I'm cool." I started walking in their direction.
"Damn man is that you?" Tray smacked his lips.
"Man, dis my cousin."
"She from 'round here?"
"She right there, talk to her." He walked over to where I was standing.
"What's up shorty?"
"Hey."
"You from 'round here?" I started smiling because I loved the way they talked down here.
"No, I'm from Ohio."
"That's why you talk so proper. So, how long you here fo'?"
"Probably until Sunday or Monday."
"Maybe I can take you out before you leave. Where are you staying?"
"With Tray."
"For real, then I'll stop by and holla at ya."
"No, moms be trippin', come by and see Tray and I'll come holla at you." We both started laughing.
"Oh, by the way they call me 'D' and you are?"
"Kya," and we shook hands.

"Nice to meet you Kya and I hope to see you in a minute."
Just as he was walking away Tray was walking my way.
"Fool, you done harassing my cousin?"
"Don't hate whotty." Tray pulled his hand out of his pocket. They gave each other five and a hug and I know they exchanged something; I just couldn't see what it was.
"I'll be by later to holla at your fine ass cousin."
"Don't get fucked up." I had started walking back to the house and Tray ran to catch up.
"Man, I know you ain't gon holla at that lame."
"He is fine."
"He is trouble."
"Why are you hanging with him then?"
"That's my brother and its business." I turned my head real fast.
"Your brother?"
"Yeah, that's my dad's son. I met him when I first came to stay with my dad last summer."
"Well, he's not related to me and I'm not trying to fuck him anyway, you know how I do it. I'm just tryna kick it." I smacked him on the back of his head and started laughing, while I took off running.

  That night about 9 pm, I was sitting in my Aunt Loren's room playing Super Mario Brothers on the Nintendo. I heard the front door close, but I didn't look back because I figured it was my mom or somebody.
"Hello ma'am." I heard a voice say.
"Hey, baby." My aunt said. I looked over my shoulder, but they had already walked past, and I was fighting the dragon on the game and about to save the princess and I wasn't trying to get out.
"That's my niece Kya."

"Oh, we've met." This time I paused the game and turned all the way around and D was standing behind me.
"Hey Boo."
"What's up?"
"Come outside and holla at me."
"Hold on let me beat this game right quick." He stood there and watched me finish the game.
"What am I missing? When did ya'll meet? Kya you haven't even been here two days." I turned around and winked at her. She shook her head and started laughing. I saved the princess and D, and I went outside on the porch.
"You're pretty good at that game."
"That's all I do at home." He kept rubbing his hands on my thighs between conversations and I would politely push his hand away. I could tell he was getting horny because he kept rubbing his penis.
"Aye walk to the park with me."
"Let me go tell my mom." I went back into the house; I knew my mom wasn't going to let me go anywhere but I tried anyway.
"Mom, I'm about to walk over to the park."
"You're not about to go anywhere. Look how dark it is outside and you don't know anybody out here."
"Tray, Antwon and Tray's brother D is out there."
"No." My aunt always tried to let me get my way.
"D is a nice young man. She'll be alright with them."
"I don't care, it's late she's not going anywhere." I went back outside to tell D.
"Mom's is trippin'."
"I heard."
"I'll holla at you tomorrow." I really had an attitude because she never let me do anything.
"You gon spend the day with me tomorrow?"

"We'll see. Call me tonight." D called me about midnight, and we talked until 4:13 am by then I was sleepy. My mom said we would probably leave Sunday night about 8:30. D said he would come and get me, Tray and Antwon around 1 pm so we could spend the day together before I left. D called me about 12:30 that afternoon and told us to meet him at the park in a half an hour. We finished getting dressed and went to the park. I was showing Tray and Antwon how to do back flips off the swings when D pulled up in this nice Mercedes all rimmed up and beating. I started getting excited.
"Tray, whose car is that?"
"Damn girl, wipe that drool off your lip, I don't know." He honked the horn.
"Come on ya'll." We all ran over and got into the car.
"Shorty, are you rollin' up front with me?" I got in the front seat. We went to the drive thru, got a fifth of Banana Red and a box of blunts then he went to this blue house, and he told us he'd be right back. He came out with a clear bottle with a clear drink inside.
"What's that?"
"Moon shine, gurl." He made a couple more stops then we went to another house.
"Hold up ya'll I locked my keys in the house. Meet me at the front door." Tray started laughing.
"What's so funny?"
"Nothing, enjoy yourself big cuz." D came and opened the front door, and he left his keys in the ignition.
"Aren't you going to get your keys out of the car?"
"Naw, they alright." He gave us all a glass and some ice; we drank the Banana Red first while we played a hand of spades, and they smoked two blunts. D passed me the Blunt.

"I don't smoke."
"Gurl, this is some fire. Try it."
"Naw, I'm cool", so I passed it to Antwon. By the end of the game, I had a real buzz.
"I have to use the bathroom."
"Come on I'll show you where it's at." When we got to the hallway out of sight from everyone else D stated tonguing me down. I was feeling good, and I was feeling him. We went into a bedroom, I know didn't belong to him because there were stuffed animals all over the bed, a glass tray sat on the dresser with, lady Stetson, white diamond and some other little bottles of ladies' perfume sitting on it. He laid me on the bed and was kissing me very passionately and grinding on me real hard. He stood up to take his pants off. I wasn't about to give him any, so I got up.
"I have to go to the bathroom."
"My bad shorty, it's the first door on the left." I went into the bathroom and relieved myself. I squatted and peed all over the seat because my aim wasn't all the good. I wiped, cleaned the seat off, fleshed the toilet, washed my hands and then decided to me nosy. I looked in the medicine cabinet and there were two combs and a brush with hair in them and D had a brush cut. There was some Pear berry body wash on the shower and in the drawer, there were Tampons. Now I know this was not his house. I checked myself in the mirror and went back into the kitchen with Tray and Antwon.
"Where is D at?"
"I don't know. I think he still back there in that room, go get him because I'm ready to go."
"We just ordered a pizza, and it won't be here for thirty minutes."

"That's cool because I am hungry." We started playing a hand of Pity Pat while we waited for D to come out of the room.
"Kya, what happened to you? Man, you trippin'. Come here and let's finish this conversation."
"Oh, I'm done talking."
"That's how you gon play me?" he shook his head up and down. "Alright."
"Do ya'll want to play another game of spades until the pizza gets here."
"I don't care", said Tray.
"This time let's switch partners D you on my team." He got up and sat across the table from me. We played two hands and the pizza arrived. We put down our cards and everybody ate their pizza and D gave us some Bush beer that was in the refrigerator.
"I think we better be getting back, it's getting late, and I don't wanna hear mom's mouth." Tray looked at his watch. "Dang, its 7:30 already. Yeah, we better get going."
"Hold up Kya let me holla at you right quick before we go." I walked back into the room with him, and he pushed me up against the wall.
"Can we finish were we left off?"
"Naw D, you are a cutie, but I don't know you like that. I don't even know your real name."
"It's Darryl, baby, I got some rubbers if that's what you're worried about."
"It's not that, I'm just…, I just can't."
"I can respect that. Why don't you give me your number and I'll give you mine and I just might surprise you and come see you one day."
"That's cool." He kissed me on the forehead.

"Now let me get you back before your mom beat the black off of you."
"Whatever." We went back into the kitchen. "Come on ya'll let's roll." We got back into the car and Darryl had the music beating listening to 2nd to none, he was going like 50 mph, and we were all kickin' it until we heard the sirens of a police car. I looked in the side window and they were behind us.
"All shit" Darryl said, "Put ya'll seatbelts on I'm about to lose this motha fucka." He turned so many sharp corners and went down so many back alleys and finally he lost them as he pulled up in the backfield of the park right by my cousin's house and drove through the grass. "Kya I'll call you; I'll holla at you lil' bro. Ya'll, get out!" He didn't have to tell me twice. I was trying to get out so fast I forgot I had my seatbelt on until it held me back. We ran all the way to my Auntie's house and when we got there my mom was putting our stuff in the van.
"Tray, what was that all about?"
"Man, you know that wasn't his car." I left it alone. I went to tell my aunt good-bye, gave Tray a hug and got into the van to head back to good old Ohio.

****

It was kind of chilly for the Middle of June when we arrived home Monday afternoon. But I didn't care, I was just glad to be home. My mom made us shake out all our clothes one piece at a time before we were aloud to bring our bags in the house. I wasn't in the mood for this I wanted to take me a long hot bath and get in my own bed and rest. I went in my room and the light on my answering machine was flashing so I pressed play.

"Hey Kya, this Mike I figured you'd be back by now. Call me when you get in. I miss you." I went and ran my bath water and then called him back, but he didn't answer the phone, so I paged him and went and took my bath. I called Otis while I was bathing but he wasn't home either, so I soaked until I was wrinkled then I went to bed.

       The phone woke me up at 5:13 pm, I was sleeping well.
"Hello." I said in a sleepy voice.
"Welcome back baby." It was Mike.
"It took you long enough to call me back."
"I was handling some business. Can I see your pretty face today?"
"I don't know I might swing by later on, I'm tired."
"Did you enjoy yourself?"
"Yes, I had a really nice time."
"That's good, well you get you some rest and I'll talk to you later." I got up to make something to eat when I heard someone at the door. I looked through the peephole and it looked like Mike, so I looked out the window and I saw his Blazer in front of my house. I opened the door and there he was standing with a box of long steamed roses. My mouth dropped and I gave him a hug. This was the first time I had ever gotten a box of roses.
"Thank you, baby,", he smiled.
"You're welcome. I missed you."
"I missed you too. Come talk to me while I fix me something to eat."
"Get dressed I'll take you to get something." I wasn't in the mood for a seat down meal, so I suggested that we go to Dairy Queen and get some burgers, that way I could get me a Cookie and Cream Blizzard.

CHAPTER- 8

Otis paged me right at 4:00 pm; I was just getting from work. Instead of calling him back I went over his house to see what was up.

"I wasn't expecting you to come over."
"Well, you were on the way. What's up?"
"Can we do something later on, like go to the movies?"
"That sounds good. What time you talking?"
"About seven or eight?"
"Alright, I'm about to go home and finish filling out my papers for the University of Akron, because I want to enroll by next spring."
"Okay, I'll see you later." We kissed and then I went home. I called Mike to get him out of the way and told him that I was going to go kick it with my girl later and I would call him when I came back.

Otis called me at 6:18 and said he was on his way. I changed into a pair of jeans and a hoodie and got out of my dress clothes. We went to see Benji, and I cried like a big baby because those movies always have a happy ending. When we returned to my house, we were lying on the couch watching television when my pager went off, it read: 111, I hit the button and kept watching TV, then my house phone rang, and I let the answering machine pick it up and they hung up. Beep, beep, beep my pager went off again this time it read: 111-411. I go downstairs to another room and call Mike back on my mother's phone.

"What's up?"
"Where you at?"
"Still over my girl's."
"When are you coming home?"

"In a little bit. Why?"
"I just asked. So how did you get over you girl's house?" I hurried to the window and looked outside, and I saw his car parked right in front of the house.
"Her mom came and got me. Why are you asking me all these questions?" I had Otis, park his car in the garage, so he didn't know I had company.
"I'm sitting outside your house, and I see your car in the driveway."
"Well why don't you come and get me, since you don't have nothing better to do." I was trying to get him to leave so that I could get Otis out of the house. "It might be a minute." I was trying to think of anything to say to get him to leave.
"I have nothing but time, so I'll be here when you get here."
"Alright," I hung up the phone and Otis and I finished watching TV hoping that Mike would just leave. About a half an hour later I heard someone putting a key in the side door and the door opened. I looked out of the side window, and it was Antwon and Mike was getting out of his car walking up behind him talking.
"Shit!"
I ran downstairs as quietly as I could and told Otis to go into my room and leave the lights off. I hid behind the door and tapped Antwon on the arm and put my finger to my lips for him not to say anything. I had enough time to run behind the table and squat down on the floor before Mike got into the house. I snuck back upstairs and Otis and I sat in my room for like ten minutes.
"Aye come on, we can sneak out of the front door while they're downstairs." Otis and I headed for the door when I heard some loud footsteps coming up the stairs fast. We

tried to get into the hall closet but it was too late Mike was in the kitchen.
"What the fuck is you doing man? I knew your bitch ass was in here." Antwon came upstairs and sat on the kitchen counter with his arms crossed over his chest just observing.
"So, you still fucking with my bitch?" He started walking towards Otis.
"Man, you better get the fuck out of his face. If you got a problem with somebody it should be me because I'm the one who invited him over here." I got between them and started pushing Mike away from him.
"I'm gon deal with you later, but I'm going to fuck this nigga up right now." I pushed Mike out of the way and Antwon signaled for Otis to come down the basement with him. Mike continued to argue with me about nothing and Antwon let Otis out the garage, and I stood against the door so that Mike couldn't get outside to try to follow him.
"Get the fuck out the way", he said while pulling on my arm, but I was pulling back with all my might. "Why you always standing up for that punk?"
"Because you're ignorant and I don't want that bull shit around me."
"Well tell him to stay the fuck away from you." Then he mugged me in my face and my head hit the door, and I pushed him into the wall.
"You better keep your fucking hands to yourself." Antwon heard the commotion, and he came back upstairs.
"Fuck you Kya", and he left. I heard his tires screeching down the street. I went into my room and called Otis the phone rang five times before he answered.
"What are you doing?"
"Does it matter?"
"Ooh, it's like that?"

"Look Kya, I don't have time for this, you need to make up your mind as to who you want to be with."
"But I…" and then I heard a dial tone. I looked at the phone like *I know he didn't*. I hung up the phone and started crying, because I didn't want to lose either one of them, but I knew right then and there that I had to choose.

CHAPTER- 9

It was a really bad snowstorm and I had woken up about 4:30 am and I called Mike to ask him to come over but he didn't answer his phone, so I paged him and put 111 in his pager, but he didn't call me back. I knew he slept on the couch and the phone was right next to it so if he was at home sleep he would have heard the phone ring, but he didn't answer. I called his cell phone still no answer, so I paged him again with 111-411. I waited about a half an hour, and he didn't call me back, so I paged him again and then I decided to get up and go over there. It took me a good five minutes to clean all the snow from my car, but that gave my car a good enough time to warm up. I slid and fish-tailed it all the way over to Mike's and the first thing that crossed my mind was *he better be home*. I pulled up in front of his house and his car was parked on the street in front of his house along with another car and his truck was in the driveway and they were both full of snow, so I knew he hadn't been anywhere. I got out of the car and knocked on the door and there was no answer than I rang the doorbell and I saw him look out the window. He came to the door fully dressed, including his shoes.
"Why you not answering your phone?"
"Because I was sleep."
"Fully dressed, with shoes on, huh?" He just looked at me.
"So... you gon let me in, it's cold out here." He sighed heavily and moved so I could get passed. When I walked through the second set of doors, I saw Cynthia sitting on the couch with a newborn baby lying beside her. I sat down in the chair across from her and Mike went into the kitchen then she followed.
"What the fuck is she doing here?"

"I didn't know, ask her."

"Well tell her she got to leave. This is supposed to be our time."

"Man, you trippin'." They stood in the kitchen and argued for about a half an hour, and then Mike came into the living room. "Come on Kya let's go." I got up out of the chair. "Where are we going?"

"Just come on." We get outside and he locked the screen door and took the keys so Cynthia couldn't leave. "I'm going to meet you at your house."

"Alright," I got into my car and drove home. I went into the house and before I could get settled in Mike called me from his cell phone.

"You ready?"

"Ready for what?"

"Just come on." I went outside and got into his car. We drove for about ten minutes, when I saw us heading down Darrow Road, I knew we were going to the Best Western Hotel, because that's where we always went when we wanted to be away from the world. We made love all morning, but his pager kept going off, so he finally got up and called his mom. Cynthia had called his mom and told her what happened and that if he didn't come back, she was going to take his necklace with his name on it because she knew that meant a lot to him. He got dressed and told me he'd be right back. I fell asleep and when I woke up, I had four missed calls on my pager. I went through the calls, and they were all from my Aunt Jazman and a 911 followed the last two so I called her back.

"What's up Jazman?"

"Girl, where you at? I've been calling you all morning."

"I'm chillin'."

"Well, your grandma is in the hospital, and I don't think that she is going to make it this time." I didn't say anything. "She wants us all at the hospital when they take her off of life support, so you can stop chillin' and get down there."

"Give me like an hour and I'll be there." I hung up the phone and paged Mike 911. He came back to the room about twenty minutes later and I was lying on the bed crying.

"What's wrong Kya?"

"I need to go home; my grandmother is in the hospital, and they don't think she's going to make it." He held me until I stopped crying and then he took me home. I took a bath, threw on a jogging suit and went to the hospital. When I got there everyone else had already arrived and was standing around her bed. I took a seat right next to her bed and then I saw a tear roll down the side of her face and I lost it. I ran into the bathroom and cried. My grandma and I were very close. My mom didn't like me staying home with the boys over the summer while she was working so I would stay with my grandma and every time I thought that my mom was being mean to me, I would call and tell my grandma and if she thought she was wrong, she would call her and say something to her. My Aunt Shelby came in the bathroom and hugged me and gave me a wet paper towel to wipe my face. I stayed in the bathroom another five minutes to compose myself, because I didn't want to make anyone else upset. When we were all there the doctor came in and we all said a prayer, then they pulled the plug. That was the first time I had ever watched anyone die.

CHAPTER- 10

My mom was in the kitchen making a pot of spaghetti when her phone rang.
"Hello."
"Hello, Mrs. Walters?"
"Yes."
"This is Mrs. Wallace, Tye's mom."
"Um hum."
"Did you know that Kya was messing around with my nephew, Mike?"
"Yeah, he calls her and comes over every now and then, why?"
"And you're Okay with that?"
"What do you mean?"
"He's twenty-five years old and Kya's only eighteen for starts, he has eight kids and one on the way and he said that Kya's going to have number ten. He sells drugs and he just, not too long ago, got out of jail because he got busted."
"He has eight kids?"
"And one on the way."
"Well Kya didn't tell me all that. I pretty much let her make her own decisions because she's grown and she has to live and learn, but I'm going to talk to her about this. Thanks for calling."
"Kya's a good kid and she doesn't need to be involved with anybody like that, she has a nice little boyfriend that she needs to keep."

    I was in my room listening to Keith Sweat.
"Kya", my mom called as she was knocking on my door.
"Huh?"

"I need to talk to you for a minute."
"You can come in."
"No, you come out." I turned down my radio and went into the living room and sat on the love seat. My mom lit a cigarette, so I knew this was something.
"Yes?"
"Mrs. Wallace just called."
"I don't even talk to Tye anymore so…"
"I didn't ask you that." I didn't respond I just looked at her. "So, is Mike supposed to be your new boyfriend?"
"We're just friends. Why?"
"Well, I didn't know that he was twenty-five, he is too old to be calling here. Aren't you supposed to be with Otis anyways? He is a nice young man and he's cute with no kids."
"I know he is cute, but he's boring, and Mike buys me everything that I want and more and half the time I don't even have to ask."
"Well baby all money isn't good money, sometimes the finer things in life can lead to a world of trouble in the future. I know I can't run your life, because you think that you're grown and you're going to do what you want to do, but you need to sit down and think about what you want to do. Look, I want you to go in your room and get a piece of paper and make two columns and put the good things in one and the faults in the other for Mike and Otis and see who comes out the best. Oh, and who is Angelica?"
"Mike's ex-girlfriend."
"Oh, she supposed to be pregnant?"
"Not that I know of. Why?"
"Well, that's what his aunt said, and she would know. And he just had a baby?", and she shook her head.

"About six months ago, but she was pregnant when I meet him."
"See, that's what I'm saying. I don't want to see him in this house again." I smacked my lips.
"Alright." I got up and went back into my bedroom and rewound my Keith Sweat tape back to *Right and Wrong Way* and paged Mike so that my phone would ring, and she would think that somebody else was just calling and not that I was running to tell Mike everything, which I was.

      I was laying across my waterbed making out my list and of course Otis came out to the better man, but I was so into Mike that the list didn't matter. I wanted Mike and that's who I was going to be with. By the time Mike called me back I had gotten depressed.
"What's up baby?"
"Nothing really, I just need to ask you a question and I need for you to be totally honest, because I'm going to find out one way or the other, but I want to hear it from you."
"What?" His mood totally changed; it sounded like he had an attitude.
"Is Angelica supposed to be pregnant by you?"
"Naw, man. Who told you that?"
"Your aunt called my mom." I told him everything that my mom had told me that his aunt said.
"She just mad and don't want us to be together."
"Mike, would you lie to me?"
"Look Kya, I love you and I would never do anything to hurt you."
"Okay"
"Aye, you want to go to Toledo with me this weekend?"
"I can't my mom's not feeling you anymore, so she's not going to let me go."

"Well, I'll leave Saturday morning and I'll have you back before it gets too late, since it's only a two-hour drive and I bowl at 11:30 in the morning, I should be done about three or four then we can go get something to eat or something."
"That sounds like a winner to me."

CHAPTER- 11

Six months later, the summer of 1995 I had not to long ago turn nineteen. Mike and I had really grown close, I would go out of town with him every weekend to his bowling tournaments or I would spend the night at his house. My mother had realized that I was going to see Mike with or without her consent and she couldn't watch my every move and she would rather me be in our house where she could watch me, then me lying and sneaking around. Mike would come over almost every other day and she would tell him to leave. This went on for a good month.
"Mike why do you keep coming around here, I told you I didn't want you seeing my daughter."
"Look Mrs. Walters, no disrespect but I love Kya and I won't do anything to hurt her, that's my baby, she makes me so happy."
"You are too old for Kya you need to be dating somebody like me." He gave her a crazy look.
"You! That's like dating my mom." She busted out laughing.
"Well, she can't have any company right now." From that day forward he was allowed over. I don't think she really liked him, but she accepted him because I did.

****

It was 2:30 Sunday morning and Mike and I went to Country Kitchen to get breakfast; we both ordered the Omelets and hash brown meal. On the ride back to his house we were listening to music when Mike turned down the volume.
"Kya, I need you to do me a favor."
"What's up?"

"I need about three thousand dollars. I'll give it back to you in two weeks."
"What makes you think I have that kind of money?"
"You got it."
"Let me see what I can do, and I'll let you know when I get home." I knew that I had it, but I didn't feel comfortable giving anybody that kind of money when I knew there was a chance he could go to jail and me not getting my money back. He took me home Sunday around 11:00 am because I needed to finish my homework and get my clothes together for work the next day. I called the bank and I had $4,022.64, so I said I would give him two thousand dollars. I took my bath and made myself a bowl of cereal then I called him back.
"I know you weren't sleep."
"Yeah, I dozed off for a minute. What's up?"
"Is two good?"
"Is that all you can get?"
"Yeah."
"Well, that's good, when can you get it?"
"Tuesday, because tomorrow I have morning and evening classes and I have to go to work. So, when I get off Tuesday, I'll be over."
"Alright."
"Well, I'm about to go in here and watch lifetime, so I'll talk to you later."
"Bye baby."

  That Tuesday as promised, I went to the bank on my lunch break and withdrew two thousand dollars in big bills. I called Mike at 4 pm when I got off work to let know I was on my way. When I got to his house Cheryl, Michelle's mom, was leaving. She along with his other baby mamas couldn't stand me for some reason or another and they didn't want me around. She stopped on the sidewalk and just stared at me with this mug on her face. I stopped and stared back at here with a look on my face like, *what?*

"Kya" Mike broke our stare. "Go in the house, I'll be in there in a minute." I went into the house and sat down on the couch and the phone rang, I didn't answer it, but I looked at the caller ID and it was Angelica. I dumped everything out of my purse trying to find a pen and wrote her number down on the back of an envelope I had in my purse. Mike walked in the door just as I was putting everything back in my purse.

"What are you doing?"

"Oh, I was looking for something." He went to the kitchen and started cooking some dope while I did my homework. I couldn't concentrate because I wanted to know what Angelica was calling for, but I didn't want to ask him. Then I heard his pager going off again, but he never called anyone back. I walked in the kitchen.

"Who is that blowing up your pager?"

"It's business." I knew he was lying.

"Well, I'm about to go."

"Why, what's wrong?"

"Nothing, I just want to go home."

"Did you get that change for me?" I went into my purse and pulled out the bank envelope and handed it to him.

"Two weeks."

"It might even be sooner than that." He kissed me on the cheek. "Thank you, baby," and I left.

CHAPTER- 12

Saturday afternoon I was sitting around watching BET when Shawn called.
"What are you doing tonight, girl?"
"Shit. Why, what's up?"
"I'm trying to go out. You down?"
"You know it."
"My cousins Gale, Tammy and Shirley are going too, so we are hanging with the big dogs tonight." Tammy and Shirley were in there late 20's early 30's, but they were cool to kick it with.
"That's cool, where are we going?"
"Some spot on the Southside called Rogers, they don't ID in there, so we should be good."
"What time should I be ready?"
"About 9:30." I started getting ready at 8:00 and by 9:15, I was looking fly. I had on a little mini skirt that showed off my long legs, a black sports bra and a black and white vest that I left open to show off my little waistline and flat stomach. I had my hair pulled out of my face and pinned up in a half bun on the right side and hanging down over my shoulders everywhere else. Surprisingly Shawn was on time because she was always late. We rode around while they smoked a blunt, then we headed to the club around 10:00. When we walked in, I had a nervous feeling in my stomach, so I sat in the back to observe the atmosphere. I ordered a Bud Ice than sat back down in the back just as Mike was walking in the door. He couldn't see me because I was sitting in the far corner behind the door, and he would never expect to see me on that side of town. It was the straight up hood. I watched as he shook hands with almost everyone in the club and they were buying him drinks. I

didn't see him go in his pocket one time. After awhile he started playing a game of pool, so I went over to say what's up.
"Hey you." He looked over his shoulder.
"What are you doing in here?"
"I came to have a drink with my girls." He looked down at my beer.
"You want something else?"
"Naw, I'm cool."
"Well, if you need anything let me know."
"Alright." I walked back over with my girl.
"You see Mike over there."
"Um hum and I see his baby mama walking through the door." I looked over and Cynthia was standing in the doorway.
"Didn't she just have a baby?"
"Yup."
"How old is it?"
"She's about five or six months."
"Dang, she didn't gain no weight." She ordered herself a drink, and then went over to watch Mike play pool.

It was getting close to midnight, and they wanted to stop by the Treetop, another hood bar on the North side. "Ya'll finish up your drinks so we can roll out." I had just ordered another beer and had only taken a few sips out of it, so I told them to give me a minute. They went outside to wait, and Cheryl walked in. She sat down at the bar and ordered herself a drink. I was half finished when Shawn walked back in.
"Come on Kya."
"Let me go tell Mike I'm leaving. I'll be right back." I walked over to the pool table.

"Aye, I'm about to go. Why don't you walk me outside so I can holla at you right quick?"
"I'm in the middle of a game, I'll call you later."
"Alri…"
"You need to get the fuck up out his face."
"Excuse me?" I turned around and Cheryl was standing behind me with her finger now pointing in my face.
"Bitch, you better get your hands up out of my face."
"What you say?"
"I said Bitch" and I paused so she could understand "you better get your hands out my face." Mike and Cynthia were standing there with their arms folded over their chests. Cheryl grabbed my hair; she was bigger than me weight and height wise. I was pushing 120 pounds and she had to be at least 180. She had my head to where I could only see the floor, so I started punching her in her sides. Then I blacked out, that's something that usually happened when I get really, really mad. When I came to, I was falling backwards over a bar stool, and she was falling on top of me. Everybody was standing in one corner of the bar. All the bar stools were knocked over and the tables were pushed everywhere, and Cheryl was still holding onto my hair. The owner was trying to pull us apart, but she wouldn't let go of my hair.
"Let go of my hair." I said in a calm voice.
"Fuck you!" and she let go. As I was getting up, I realized that my breast was hanging out and my panties were showing. I was glad I didn't put on any granny draws. I fixed my clothes and started fixing my hair when Cheryl came behind me with a beer bottle. Mike ran over and snatched it out of her hand.
"Man, don't do that shit."

The owner of the club was furious. "Everybody get the fuck out, we're closed." He knew I wasn't old enough to be in there, but he let all the cute girls with tight pants and short skirts on in. I was pissed at Shawn because she just stood there and watched, it wasn't that I was getting my ass beat, because she didn't get any hits in, it was just when we fell over the bar stools, she fell on top of me. She could have gotten me good, but she didn't. I went up to Mike "Oh and don't think I was fighting over you because I wasn't. I was fighting because that bitch got in my face." "Whatever." My girls and I left and went to the Treetop.

On the ride there everybody wanted to talk about what happened. "Dang, ya'll tore that whole bar up in three minutes", said Gale.
"Yeah, all I had time to do was smoke me a cigarette", said Shirley. They were all hyped about it, but I didn't want to talk about it, all I wanted to do was go home.

I paged Mike about six times Sunday night and fell asleep waiting on him to return my call. I woke up Monday morning to my alarm clock. I got dressed and went over Mike's house about 7 am and banged on the door for about twenty minutes. I knew he was in there because his cars were outside, and his keys were still in the door, and he couldn't have locked the door from the outside without those keys. I was knocking so hard that the neighbors came out, but Mike never answered.

I had a key to Mike's Maximum, and I knew his alarm was always set so I unlocked the door and opened it to set the alarm off, but he still didn't come to the door.

When the alarm stopped, I started banging on the door again, then I heard some kids talking.
"Daddy, somebody's at the door." Cheryl opened the door and came on the porch. I smacked my lips.
"Where is Mike?"
"He's asleep."
"Tell him he has company."
"I'm not telling him nothing, you need to leave." Now I was getting pissed.
"Fuck you! Don't tell me what I need to do."
"You better leave before I come out there and make you, ain't nobody here to break it up this time."
"There's nothing between us but space and opportunity baby." I looked up at her and her right eye was bloodshot red and swollen. My girl had told me I caught her with a good right hook, but I didn't think much of it.
"You know what I don't have time for this."
I chuckled "I bet you don't. You can have Mike because I don't want his tired ass, just tell him to give me my money back."
"Whelp, you shouldn't have given it to him, he's going to spend that on me and my kids." Then she slammed the door. I picked up a brick and throw it at the door, but he had a security door, so it just made a lot of noise and then hit the ground. I got into his car and the alarm went off again. I was going to leave in it, but that meant that I had to leave my car over there. I got into my car and went to class. I had a math test anyway.

When I got off work, I went to get my Auntie Jazman. She was in her early thirties, but she and I hung out a lot and she had won the Golden Gloves in Michigan, and she was down for whatever. We went over Mike's, and

he was outside with his daughter and Cheryl's other kids. I got out of the car and walked over to where he was standing.
"I need my money."
"Man, don't come at me like that."
"I'm not playing with you; give me my money and I'm done." He looked down at my car to try to make out who was sitting in it.
"Who is that?"
"Don't worry about it."
"Well, I'll get it to you when I can." For the next week and a half Mike called me everyday I just told him flatly, if he wasn't calling about my money there was no need for us to talk. By the end of the second week, he gave me my money back.

CHAPTER- 13

I woke up to someone banging on the door, I looked at the clock and it read 7:24. "Awe shit!" I jumped out of the bed. I had overslept. I ran and opened the door and I saw it was Mike, so I ran into the bathroom to start getting ready for work. He stood in the doorway of the bathroom and just looked at me.
"What you want?" He just smiled at me. "Whaaat… your girlfriend let you out of the house."
"That's not my girlfriend."
"Don't ya'll live together?"
"No, she's staying there because her electric is cut off and I'm not going to let them kids live like that."
"Well keep the kids and make her leave."
"Man, I can't do that."
"You just don't want to do that, in house pussy, how convenient."
"Man whatever, if that's what you think then you can come stay down there too and see for your self."
"Thanks, but no thanks I'm not into that freaky shit." He came into the bathroom, stood behind me, put his arms around my waist and was looking in the mirror.
"We're going to have us a pretty baby."
"Um" he started kissing me on the back of my neck.
"Gone boy, I'm already running late for work." We continued to talk while I got dressed.
"Can I come have lunch with you today?"
"I don't care." We had lunch and he called me every morning to tell me good morning and have to a nice day, every afternoon to see how my day was going and every night to tell me good night. After a week or so of that we were back together, and I was in love all over again.

CHAPTER- 14

It was the day before Thanksgiving. I had been over Mike's all day and his pager had been blowing up, but he never called anyone back. He had turned the ringer off his house phone because every now and then I would see the light on the phone light up. "I'm about to go home and help my mom get things ready for tomorrow."
"Man don't go over there and mess the food up cause I gotta eat that too."
"Yeah, I'm going to make you a special plate." We started laughing; I put on my coat and started walking towards the door. I went outside and when I got to the sidewalk a car pulled up really fast and slammed on the brakes, '*eeerrrrr*' I stopped in my tracks because I knew his baby's mamas were on some bull shit. They didn't like me because they said, "*I thought that I was the shit,.*" but I think they were just jealous because I was way younger than them and had a better car, better job, no kids and was going to school and Mike was into me and most of the time put me before them. To my surprise Tye jumped out of the car. "I thought I told you to stay the fuck away from my cousin." *I'm not in the mood for this.* I said to myself. I just looked at her with my left eye squinted and my mouth to the side like whatever. Then I looked up and her sister was walking up the driveway. I knew they were down for jumping people and I was not prepared. Mike ran over to where we were standing. "Tye, man what the fuck you doin'?"
"Mike, why are you fucking with this raggedy bitch."
"Man, get the fuck out of here before I whip your ass." I looked at her and smiled, and that just pissed her off because Mike was on my side.

"Don't worry about it, I'll catch you. Mike won't always be around."
"Kya go back in the house; I'll be in there in a minute."
"I'm about to go home."
He gave me a pleading look. "Please."
"Don't beg that bitch."
"Would you shut the fuck up?" I laughed again and went back into the house and sat on the couch and waited for Mike. Mike and Tye were outside for another twenty minutes. I kept hearing Mike getting loud, but I couldn't make out what he was saying. I called my mom. "Hey, how are you coming on dinner?"
"It'll be done by the time you get here."
"I'll be there in a bit." Mike walked in as I was hanging up the phone. "I'm sorry about that baby." He was mad. He sat down on the couch beside me and picked up the phone and called somebody.
"Aye, I need you to do me a favor, its a hundred dollars riding on it too. You know that little bitch Tamika across the street from me? I want you to beat the fuck out of her." He paused. "She all in my business, keeping shit going. She don't even know you. Who Tye? Naw, I guess her, and Tye supposed to be cool." He paused for a good minute. "Okay, I'll see you then. Good looking out." He hung up the phone.
"What was that all about?"
"Tamika called and told Tye you were over here. She calls her every time you come over here, so I got somebody to beat her ass."
"You don't need to pay nobody to beat her ass. I'll do it."
"I don't want you out here fighting, and they'll probably try to jump you, and I don't feel like going back to jail for beating no bitch's ass for messing with my baby." I started

smiling. I was really beginning to fall in love with him. Then he kissed me on the cheek. We talked for another hour or so.

"Let me get out of here. My mom is going to cuss me out."

"Yeah, I don't want you getting in no trouble." He got up to walk me outside when somebody knocked on the door. "Hold up let me see who this is." He looked out the door window. "Fuck." I gave him a distraught look. "I'm not answering that. I don't even feel like being bothered, so you might as well have a seat until they leave."

"Who is that?"

"Trouble," I assumed it was Tye and her sister again, so I sat back down. They started ringing the doorbell and banging on the door and blowing the horn in their car. He kept peeking at them out of the window. They had been out there for fifteen minutes. "I'll be right back, let me go handle this." Mike left and when he got outside, I heard him arguing with somebody and it wasn't Tye's voice, so I looked out of the window, and it was Angelica. Now I was ready to leave, but I was kind of scared because she wasn't by herself, and I thought he had locked me in, so I waited. Ten minutes later the light on the phone lit up. I looked at the caller ID and it was a private number, so I didn't answer it. Then my pager went off and it read 111, then the light on the phone lit up again, this time I answered. "Why are you answering my phone?"

"Why are you calling here?" I was relieved but mad at the same time. "You can go ahead and go home. I'll call you later."

"Where you at?"

"Over my mom's."

"How am I going to get out?" He started laughing. "I left the key in the door and locked it with my other one. So just take it with you and I'll get it later." I jogged outside checking my surroundings and got in my car, I didn't even turn around; I bagged up all the way to the corner and headed home. When I pulled in my driveway, I heard this thumping sound. I got out of the car, and I had a flat tire. "Auggg." I counted to ten and went in the house. My mom was down the basement, so I went upstairs and paged Mike 911 and went to wash my hands. He called right back.
"Who was that who came to your house?" I already knew the answer; I just wanted to see if he was going to lie.
"Why?"
"Because I got a flat tire."
"I'll fix it in the morning, don't worry about it."
"Don't worry…"
"Kya?" My mom called from the kitchen.
"I'll call you back" and I hung up the phone.

    It was 7:30 Thanksgiving morning my mom busted in my bedroom. "Kya, get up."
"For what, it's only seven thirty."
"Mike is outside doing something to your car."
"He's probable fixing my tire. I had a flat."
"How did that happen?"
"I don't know."
"Um, well you need to get up and go out there", and she slammed my bedroom door. I got up and put on a pair of sweatpants and went outside. Mike had just finished putting a can of fix-a-flat in my tire, but you could hear the air seeping back out.
"So that didn't work?"

"Ah", he jumped. "Don't walk up on me like that. You are going to have to follow me down to the tire shop so you can get a new one or get this one patched."
"I have a warranty on them at Goodyear, so it just might be free."
"Well come on before all of the air is gone again."
"Let me grab my ID." I ran in the house and brushed my teeth real quick and grabbed my driver's license.
"Mom I'll be right back; I'm going down to Goodyear to get a new tire." Mike followed me to Goodyear and the tire was slashed and couldn't be repaired. He had to come up off fifty-four dollars and thirty-five cents he paid them with at hundred-dollar bill, and he kissed me on my lips. "I gotta go, I'll call you later." When I got home it was close to nine am. I took my bath, got dressed and helped my mom with the last preparations for Thanksgiving dinner.

CHAPTER- 15

Wednesday morning about 3 am my phone rang, I looked at the clock again to make sure I saw it right and it read 3:13. *This better be important*, I said to myself.
"Hello?" I said with an attitude.
"Kya."
"What?"
"I just got pulled over and they about to take me to jail."
"For what?" I sat up in my bed.
"Some bull shit. Call my mom and let her know what's going on. I'll call you back when I get booked."
I hung up the phone and called his mom. "Hello Mrs. Mack, this is Kya, sorry to call you so late but Mike asked me to call and tell you he's in jail."
"For What?"
"I don't know he said he'd call me back when he gets booked."
"Well, I don't have any money to get him out."
"Well, I do, just let me know."
"Okay thanks for calling." I hung up the phone and just laid there and stared into the darkness until my alarm went off at 6:15am. I got up and started getting ready for work and at 6:58 the phone rang. I ran to my room dripping toothpaste out of my mouth, onto the carpet. "Hello." And the operator came on:
"You have a collect call from." Then it paused.
"Trouble."
"An inmate at Summit County Jail, the cost for this call is one dollar and eighty cents." I already knew the procedure because Mike had been down this road one time too many, so I pressed one.
"Hey bay."

"What happened?"
"Man, that bitch went down there and told them folks that I jumped on her and that I had drugs in my house."
"Who?"
"Cheryl."
"Why did she do that?"
"Because she stupid."
"Well, did you?"
"Man, I didn't touch that bitch. They came and searched my house, but they only found a scale and some residue, so I'm not worried."
"Oh. Well, what did the police say?"
"They were cool, I have to go to court tomorrow morning and I go from there." We talked until the operator came on again.
"You have one minute left to talk."
"Alright, call and let me know what happens tomorrow in court."
"I will baby, I love you."
"I love you too." Mike ended up getting six months in the Oriana House.

CHAPTER- 16

I went to pick up my cousin Latoya, because we worked together, and we figured car pulling would save us both some money. I pulled in front of her house and blew the horn. She came out with her make up kit in her hand and got into the car.

"Overslept?" I asked looking at her face without makeup.
"Yeah, I forgot to set my alarm last night."
"I was talking to Mike this morning; his dumb ass done got locked up. I just knew I was going to be running late."
"You still mess with him?"
"Yeah, that's my Boo."
"Did you know that Angelica is supposed to be pregnant?"
"Who told you that?"
"Tye."
"Now that's the second time I have heard that. I asked Mike and he said it wasn't true."
"All I'm gone say is, be careful and keep your eyes open."

*****

Mike had scheduled me to visit him every Sunday afternoon because he said that he could only have two visitors a week and his mom, sisters, and baby's mom's all took turns with the other day. On my second visit, I was flirting with the guy at the desk and making conversation so he would remember me. On my third visit when I signed out, I went through the visitor's book and looked up all of Mike's visits from the past week and sure enough Angelica was on there for Saturday's at 2:00 pm. The guy at the desk was the same guy that was there the last week he saw what I was doing and just turned his head.

The next Saturday just couldn't come fast enough. I got dressed to impress, but not over doing it. I put on a pair of black Levi Jeans a Maroon hoodie, an all-black vest on top and my black and white Fila's that Mike had brought us alike from Cincinnati. I added my necklace with my name on it along with the diamond cut necklace that Mike had brought me for Christmas. I topped it off with the big dollar sign ring that Mike had given me plus all my own. I got to the Oriana house at 1:45 and waited in the parking lot. Angelica pulled up in Mike's Lincoln he had just brought two months ago, and it was all rimmed out with Dayton's and my stomach instantly dropped. She got out of the car stomach big as hell. I was so hurt I couldn't even cry. I let her walk ahead of me, so she could sign in first and I could get her address. When I got to the desk the same guy that usually is there on Sunday was there.
"Hey, what's up?"
"Hello. You're here a day early."
"I know, because I'm not going to be able to make my visit tomorrow and I really want to see him this week."
"Alright, just this one time. Do you have your ID?" I pulled out my driver's license and he put them in the slot. Angelica looked at me out of the corner of her eyes and kind of chuckled under her breath. We stood outside the door waiting for the inmates to come down. I stood outside on the side of the wall so Mike wouldn't see me until he came through the glass doors. Once they let them through, we had to go through the metal detectors. I got ahead of her so she could see that Mike and I had the same new shoes that they didn't sell in Akron and that I had on his rings. My back was turned to her, but when I put my hand up to hold the door for her, I heard her smack her lips. Mike was looking through the window just smiling away,

he still hadn't seen me because by now I was in the doorway, but he could see Angelica. When I walked around the corner his eyes got big.

"What the fuck is she doing here? I didn't sign her up for a visit today."

"Well, Mr. Mack she must be on the visitors list", said one of the guards.

"Well, I don't want her in here."

"Oh Mike, so that's how you doin' it? You lying bastard. Oh, and I see she is pregnant by you; you are so full of shit. Bitch, lose my number, and I mean it."

"Okay ma'am, it's time for you to go."

"Oh, I'm leaving." I was hurt. I went to get my ID and I went outside and sat in my car until Angelica came out from her visit, which was a half an hour. When she came out, I had pulled my car next to his.

"Angelica" she turned around and looked at me.

"Yes?"

"You supposed to be pregnant by Mike?"

"I sure am."

"That's all I wanted to know, tell him it's over." I got back into my car and drove over to my cousin Shatoya's house. Me, her and her sister Marleya went and got a bottle of Banana Red, and then we went to the basketball game. When the game was over it was still early, and I wasn't ready to go home.

"What ya'll want to do now."

"What's jumping that we can all get into?" asked Marleya.

"Let's go to Stonehedge's." That was a bowling alley with a game room, a bar and a food court. That was where most of the guys our age hung out that wasn't into the bar atmosphere. I was in the arcade playing Ms. Pacman when this guy walked up behind me.

"I got next."
"Um hum" and I continued to play. I was just about to clear the board when the ghosts cornered me, and I got out.
"Got damn it!" I looked over at him and smacked my lips
"Would you move?"
"My bad love" and he moved over. I just rolled my eyes because I only had one man left and I needed to clear two more boards to flip the game over. He kept standing there talking to his boy; I couldn't hear what they were talking about because I was concentrating on my game. He elbowed me.
"Ain't that right?" I turned my head to look at him.
"What?" When I turned back to my game the ghost was coming right toward me. I tried to go the other way, but I was too slow.
"Ugh" I said while gritting my teeth and I walked away.
"Baby, relax it's just a game."
"Why are you bothering me?"
"Baby don't act like that; you are too cute to have that ugly attitude." I just looked at him. "Let me take you to get something to eat. You seemed a little tensed, maybe we talk about it." I chuckled and gave him a half smile.
"No thanks." I went and found Shatoya and Marleya; they were playing the bowling game.
"Ya'll about ready?"
"In a few minutes."
"What ya'll wanna do now?"
"I'm hungry." When I thought about it, I hadn't eaten all day.
"Me too." Then those guys walked back past.
"You sure shorty? We 'bout to roll out."
"You know what…. I'm going take you up on that offer."
"I thought you were about to cuss me out."

"I apologize, man, I had a bad day."
"It couldn't have been that bad."
"I just found out the guy I've been totally committed to for the past year and a half got a baby on the way and I seen it with my own eyes and heard if from the horses mouth."
"Ouch."
"Yeah."
"Well name the place you want to eat and we're there."
"I'm rolling with my cousins here" and I pointed to Marleya and Shatoya.
"That's cool they can roll too, because I got my boys here."
We went to Swenson's since it was right next door. I followed them in my car, and we parked next to each other.
"Aye" one of the guys called as he got out of the car. I rolled down my window. "Can we get our food to go?"
"That's cool with me."
"Let's go get a room or something and just chill."
"Hold on." I rolled my window back up. "Marleya ya'll gamed?"
"Yeah" I rolled my window back down.
"Alright, we'll follow ya'll over there."
"Do ya'll want something to drink?"
"Yeah, I need one. We're drinking whatever ya'll drink."
"Do ya'll smoke?"
"I don't, but they do." We ordered our food and followed them to the State Road Inn. They put the room in their names, and we had to sign in because it was seven of us and they only allowed four to a room. We signed in under some bogus names and went upstairs, ate our food, drank up all their liquor and they smoked about three blunts with them.

I was sitting on the bed talking to the guy that messed up my game.
"By the way what is your name?"
"Oh shit, my name is Mel, Kya, right?"
"Yeah, and thanks for the food, I hadn't realized that I hadn't eaten all day." I was telling him what had happen at the Oriana house when I heard everybody start laughing. I looked back and Shatoya was lying on the floor with one of Mel's friends.
"Hold up." I got up and started walking toward the bathroom. "Toya, let me holla at you right quick." We get into the bathroom, and she gives me this dumb look.
"What the fuck are you doing? Man, you don't even know that nigga."
"They call him Bubba." I rolled my eyes, and somebody knocked on the door.
"Yeah?" It was Bubba.
"Can I come in?"
"We're having a girl talk." He changed his voice to sound like a girl.
"Well, I'll just fit right in because I need to change my tampon too." I started laughing.
"You stupid, man here we come." I turned my attention back to Shatoya. "Look, when I say I left my phone in the car, say you'll walk me outside and we out. Marleya know what's up, she'll follow suit."
We went back to the room and sat there for another five to ten minutes.
"Ah shoot!"
"What's wrong?"
"I left my phone in the car and I need it in case my mom tries to call me. I'll be right back."
"I'll walk you outside" said Shatoya.

"Ya'll ain't leaving me up here by myself", and Marleya got up and started walking toward the door. We got in the hallway and took off running. We got into the car and pulled off. I dropped my cousins off and went home to deal with the reality. I went to check my answering machine to see if Mike tried to call me. I didn't want to talk to him, but I wanted to know what he had to say, but he hadn't called so I walked to the store and bought a pack of cherry blend Black and Milds and I took the long way back and cried all the way home. When I got home my mom, and her boyfriend were there. I dried my eyes and tried to walk through the kitchen with my head down so my mother wouldn't know that I had been crying. I got halfway there.
"Where you been?"
"I walk to the store."
"This time of night?"
"I need to get something off of my chest." When she looked at me, she saw that my eyes were red.
"Come here." She took me into the garage. "Where you been all day?"
"With Shatoya and Marleya, we went to the basketball game and then to Stonehedge's."
"Then why were you crying?"
"I really don't want to talk about it." I tried to hold back my tears, but I broke down crying. I cried so hard that I fell to my knees.
"Kya, talk to me." I just kept crying. "Look go to your room and I'll be in there in a minute." I went in my room and lay across my bed for a while. I got up and freaked two mild's and went outside the front door and smoked them. My mom finished talking to her boyfriend and then he left, and I came back into the house. I heard my mom get on the phone.

"Hey, how you doing? Is Marleya or Shatoya there? No, nothings wrong." She paused for a minute. "Hey this is your auntie. What's wrong with Kya? She came in here all upset. You sure? Oh, did she? Okay, thanks." She came back into my room. I tried to act like I was asleep, but it didn't work.
She sat on the side of my waterbed and put her hand on my shoulder.
"So, what happened when you went to see Mike today?"
"Angelica was down there."
"And?" I didn't say anything. "She's pregnant, isn't she?" I shook my hand yes and tears just streamed down my face.
"Well Kya I'm not going to say I told you so, but you need to just go on with your life. He's too old for you anyway." That really was not the answer that I was looking for but I just said "Okay" so we could get off the subject and I could go to sleep because I had a headache.

CHAPTER- 17

"Good morning," Mike said when I answered the phone. I just hung up. I knew it was twenty-five cents a call, but I didn't care. He called right back, and I did the same thing. This went on for a good week. I just couldn't understand how Mike could do this to me. For the first week after I found out about Angelica, I barley ate or slept at night. I would go to the park every evening by myself to shoot some baskets or I would go feed the ducks just to clear my head. I missed Mike so much and I wanted to talk to him, but then again, I didn't. I wanted an explanation.

My phone rang Friday morning on schedule like it did every morning and as usual it was Mike.
"Kya, please don't hang up." I didn't say anything; I just held the phone to my ear. "Baby, I miss you so much." I started feeling a lump come to my throat. "And baby I love you. I am so sorry I never meant to hurt you." It sounded like he was crying, and I was a sucker for tears, and then tears began to trickle down my cheeks. I had so much I wanted to say, but I was speechless.
"Kya, please say something, don't just ignore me." Then he started crying hard. "Kya, I love you." I was glad that he was hurt because I was too.
"Mike, how could you play me like that, I gave up everything for you and I've been in your corner one hundred percent."
"I know and I'm sorry, baby. I thought you were still into your little boyfriend, and I didn't think me, and you were going to make it this far, but now I see we really got something special and…"
"We had something special."

"Don't do this baby, let's work this out."
"I don't think so." I paused for a few seconds. "Aye, I gotta go", and I hung up the phone. I felt so good because I knew he was hurt, and I was able to talk to him and let him know he had messed up. I felt relieved.

****

That evening Shawn came and picked me up. We rode around mostly on the Westside getting numbers. I even got this guy named Gabe to buy us dinner.
"See Kya, you haven't lost your skills, you don't have to settle for that nigga. I know that you love him and all, but he has put you through way too much and you don't deserve this. I've seen your type and you can do better. What's up with Otis? Ya'll still talk?"
"Yeah, every now and then, but I don't want to keep running back to him every time things go wrong with Mike and then him and Mike get into it, and I feel like it's my fault, so I try to keep the peace."
"I feel you. What are you doing tonight?"
"You know I don't have a life anymore."
"Well, we are going to the club tonight so be ready about ten." She dropped me off at home and I went in and took a nap.

My phone rang at about 8:45. "I know you're not sleep."
"Naw, I'm up. What's up?" I was lying, I was knocked out.
"Are you still going out with me?"
"Yeah, I'm about to start getting dressed in a few minutes."
"When you get done, meet me at my house." I knew that meant that I had to drive, but I didn't mind, that way I

could leave when I wanted to. I made a hamburger and some French fries and took my shower, put on some low rider jeans, a body shirt and my tennis shoes, just in case something jumped off I would be prepared.

    I got to Shawn's house just a little before 10 pm.
"I'm about to get in the shower right now."
"I knew you weren't going to be ready. I don't even know why I was rushing."
"I'll be ready in twenty minutes; my clothes are already ready, and my hair is already done." I sat down and watched T.V. with her little brothers and sisters and by ten till eleven Shawn was ready. When we got into the bar, I saw a couple of new faces that I hadn't seen the last few times I had been there. It was this one guy that was sitting in the back of the club, and he caught my eye as soon as I walked in the door. I took a seat at the bar.
"What can I get for you beautiful ladies?"
"Let me get a shot of eighteen with a lemon and a Bud Ice and give her what ever she wants." He served us our drinks.
"Come on girl let's toast, to my freedom."
"I feel you girl." We tapped our glasses and took our shots of eighteen hundred to the head then sucked our lemons.
"Uh that was well deserved." I looked over to the guy sitting in the back of the club and he was looking our way.
"Aye, look at ole dude over there with the red Polo shirt on, he is fine." The bar tender overheard my comment.
"That's my son, and don't get him in any mess." He knew I messed with Mike, and he knew how he was about his women.
"That's your least worry. I don't mess with him anymore."
"That's what your mouth say."

"What you mean by that?" He just walked away and looked at me out of the corner of his eye. Shawn and I looked at each other and shrugged our shoulders.
"He must know…"
"All of the things your man won't do, I'll do them for you." I turned around and the guy with the red shirt on from the back of the club was behind me singing and this was one of my favorite songs. I turned around and smiled. "What's up with you, do you mind if I sit here."
"I sure don't."
"Yeah, I saw you checking me out."
"No, that was you", and I started smiling.
"So, you gotta man?"
"Not anymore." Then the bartender came over to where we were sitting.
"Remember what I said." I just looked at him.
"What is he talking about?"
"I don't know, but back to what you were talking about."
"So do you have a number?" I wrote down my pager number on a napkin and handed it to him. "Well, I'm not going to bug you, so you enjoy yourself and I'll call you later." Shawn and I closed the bar as usual and we ended our evening.

CHAPTER- 18

"*Age ain't nothing but a number*." I woke up to the sound of Aaliyah's voice because I forgot to turn off my alarm clock. I got up singing with her, I made some pancakes and sausages, then took my shower and got dressed. I put on a pair of daisy dukes and a tank top because I was feeling sexy. My phone rang around 12:30.
"What up Kya?"
"What's crack-a-lackin'?"
"You sound like you in a good mood today."
"I was slippin' on my pimpin' baby, but I'm back in the game."
"Well get dressed, we're about to go riding."
"I'm already dressed, so what time are we leaving?"
"Whenever, I still gotta get dressed though."
"How are you going to call me and tell me to get ready and you're not even ready."
"All I have to do is take my shower. By the time you get here I'll be done."
"Yeah Okay," I went outside and washed my car because I knew Shawn was going to be all day. I found 'Mr. Ice Cream Man' by Master P, because I liked to ride through the projects with my fifteen inch woofers, which I had gotten hot off the streets for a hundred dollars and Mike had brought the box for them to fit into and hooked them up for me, and watch the kids think that the ice cream man was coming and they would all run outside looking around trying to find the ice cream truck and I would just laugh and laugh. I got to Shawn's house and of course she wasn't ready.

"Kya, can you go around on seventh and pick up Tina?" Tina was one of Shawn's friends, who I thought was gay, but she didn't believe me.
"Are you going to be ready when I get back?"
"Yeah."
"Man, she better be ready because I'm not going in her house, I'm not in the mood for no funny shit." We both started laughing, but I was serious. Tina was ready, we returned to Shawn's, and she still wasn't ready.
"Where are we going?"
"Just riding."
"My cousins and them want to go too."
"That's cool." We went to pick up her cousins and it was about five of them.
"Ya'll not about to squeeze up in my car, Lanay you got a car. Why don't ya'll just follow us?" She sat there for a minute and finished smoking her blunt and then she went to get her keys. We followed them to the Westside, down through the Valley and then we went to the mall. We created this game called "Who's the biggest pimp", because the streets were filled with fine jellies. By the end of the day, I had twenty-seven numbers. I would separate them by the ones I would call, they would go in my front pocket and the one's I would call only when no one else was available went in my back pocket and the one's I would never call went over my sun visor. I needed this, I had a "fuck him" attitude toward Mike and this game just reminded me that I could still have anybody I wanted. When I got home, I went through the numbers in my pockets, the pager numbers automatically got thrown in the cigar box, where I kept my rainy-day numbers. I ended up only calling seven of them. Three of them got a second call and only one got a date and we ended up dating. His name

was Marlon and he stayed with his grandmother to help her out. He sold weed, but I didn't care because that was common for guys my age. We talked on the phone late almost every night and every weekend we did something like go to the movies, played cards with my cousins and his friends or just sat around the house with him grandmother. After a month or so he was ready to get him some, but I just couldn't, I liked him a lot, but every time he tried, I would think of Mike and I felt guilty, so I would always make an excuse.

    One evening Marlon paged me right before I left work.
"What's up Kya?"
"You."
"Why don't you come see me when you get off?"
"I can do that."
"Alright I'll see you when you get here." I arrived at Marlon's about 5:20 and when I walked in the door, I could see a red and a blue light on down in the basement. He kissed me on the lips and grabbed my hand and led me down into the basement. He had the couch all made up with covers; he just knew he was about to get some. We sat down on the couch, and he leaned me back and started kissing me while he slowly unzipped my shirt. He started trying to put his hand down my pants and I grabbed his arm.
"What's the matter baby?" he asked.
"I'm not ready yet."
"Baby, it's been over a month, and I haven't been with anybody else."
"Neither have I."

"Well, we both overdue, so what's up?" He didn't wait for me to answer he just started sucking on my breast. I was enjoying it so much I didn't feel him put his hand down my pants until I felt his finger go inside me. He was breaking me down. He pulled out a condom and his son walked downstairs. *Saved by the bell,* I thought. His son was about three or four, he was standing there with his mouth open because my shirt was opened, and Marlon had his shirt off showing off that fine body and all his tattoo's and his pants were unbuttoned. I pushed his head off my breast.
"Aye, your son," I looked over at him while I covered myself.
"Go upstairs, little man with your grandma."
"Daddy, I want you."
"I'll get you in a minute. Go back upstairs." He continued to stand there.
"Go tend to your son, I have to go anyway."
"Just give me a minute."
"No, I have to go", and I got up and left. I liked Marlon, but he just wasn't Mike. I still loved Mike and I wanted him back, but I knew I had to make him suffer. I wasn't insecure and I knew I could have pretty much anybody I wanted, but I wanted Mike, because I believed in him. He had taken me places and showed me things that nobody else took the time to do. It seemed like every man that meant anything to me disappointed me in some way. Otis was a good man, but he was too good, and I didn't appreciate him and when I lost him, I learned the true meaning of love, then I met Mike, and he was every young girl's fantasy. He was seven years older than me, and I hadn't done much because I was fresh out of high school, and he took me places I never imagined. He gave me everything I wanted and needed physically, mentally and

financially. He not only showed me love but he gave me sexual healing. I actually think I was sprung.

****

"Come open the door." Mike was sitting outside in front of my house. *I might as well get it over with,* I thought. I opened the door and Mike came in the house and held me in his arms.
"I miss you baby." I pushed him off me and sat down on the couch and he began to walk towards my bedroom. I hurried up from the couch and followed him because he was good for rambling through my stuff. I sat on the edge of the bed, while he stood in front of me and just stared at me. "Kya, you just don't know how much you mean to me."
"If I meant so much to you, how could you play me like that?"
"I'm sorry baby and I'm going to do right, I promise."
"What about Angelica and the baby?"
"I'm going to take care of mine, but I don't mess with her anymore."
"Well why she still got your car?" He sighed heavily.
"She needed a way to work and to the doctors and I can't take her, so...", and he shrugged his shoulders.
He pushed me back onto the bed slowly by my shoulders. I had on my robe, because I had just gotten out of the shower, and he tried to untie it. I crossed my legs at the ankles so he couldn't try anything. He started to kiss me on my lips, and I turned my head still holding my rope strings. He put his hands up the sides of my robe and started rubbing on my hips. He started kissing me on my legs and then up to my thighs and I began to get moist, but I knew I had to stay focused. I went ahead and let him open my

robe and I scooted back on the bed and put my heels on the edge of the bed so he could get a full view. He got up to take off his pants.

"You want some don't you?" I asked him in a seductive tone.

"Um hum." He was so hard that I could see his member moving through his pants. I smiled at him.

"Well, I just wanted you to get a good look at what you gave up." I rolled off the side of the bed and ran into the bathroom to put my clothes on. He tried to follow me, but I locked the door.

"Baby, don't do me like this." I just continued to get dressed. When I came back into my room, he was laying across my bed with his pants still unbuttoned, he was massaging himself. I ignored him and went into the kitchen to eat my breakfast. He came out of my room and walked out the front door.

"Where are you going?"

"Home," I got up to lock the door and I looked outside, and his car wasn't there.

"How did you get here?"

"I got dropped off."

"Well, I'll take you home." That was my problem, I always felt sorry for people.

"That's alright, I'll walk. I need some time to think." Mike's house was almost ten minutes from mine driving, so that was a long walk.

"Are you sure, I'm about to leave?" He slammed the door and looked back at me with tears in his eyes. I felt sorry for him because I knew he was hurt, but he deserved this pain for what he had put me through. I finished my breakfast and went on with my day feeling like I had done the right thing.

CHAPTER- 19

"Good morning." My phone rang on schedule the next morning. "Were you still asleep?"
"No, I'm up. What's up?"
"These mutha fuckas tried to play me this morning. I didn't get out of here until 7:05 and now I missed the bus. Can you come and get me? It's raining hard as hell out there and I don't want to walk, and I have to get out of here before they say I can't leave."
"Angelica got your car, why don't you have her come get you?"
"Man... don't start. Are you coming or what?"
"I'm on my way."
"I'll be on that first side street across the street from the visitor's doors." When I got there, Mike was standing outside soak and wet. I unlocked the door and he got into the car.
"Where are you going?"
"Take me to my mom's, so I can get my car." We pulled into his mom's driveway, he kissed me on the lips and all those old feelings started coming back.
"I love you baby." I didn't say anything. "Oh, I got something for you come in for a minute." I followed him into his mother's house, and he disappeared around the corner as I stood by the door. He returned with his diamond cut necklace with his name on it and put it over my head. It hung all the way down to my chest and it looked good on me. "I want you to know that I'm for real." He held me in his arms, and I was in love all over again.

****

Four months later.

"Kya, I need a ride can you come and get me about 12 o'clock."
"Where are you going to be?"
"At the doors you pick me up from everyday." Every morning I had started picking Mike up and taking him over his moms to get his car, just so that I could see his face and make sure Angelica wasn't around him.
 I arrived at the Oriana house at five minutes to twelve and Mike didn't end up coming out until 12:17 and he came out caring two big black trash bags. My heart dropped.
"Where are you going with all that stuff?" He just smiled.
"Take me to my mom's." We drove to his mom's house, and I sat in the driveway waiting for him to come out.
"Why don't you come in while I take my stuff in the house so I can wash it?" I hesitated, but after a minute I got out and followed him into the house. His mom was sitting on the couch watching T.V. He gave her a hug and a kiss.
"Hey, Kya," she said while giving me a big smile.
"Hello."
"I haven't seen you in a while. What you been up to?"
"Just working and going to school."
"You are staying out of trouble?"
"I don't get in trouble." We all started laughing then her and Mike went into there own conversation while I watched whatever she was watching on the television.
"Kya, you ready?" I gave him a confused look.
"Where are we going?"
"I want some real food; let's go get something to eat." I didn't want to go because I was supposed to be with Marlon, but for some reason I felt obligated. We went to our favorite restaurant and ate well. I had the sampler,

which included ribs, cheese sticks, quesadillas, the whole nine and I had a Mucho Mudslide to drink. We ate our food as we talked.
"Man, I'm full, so you know what that means."
"You're sleepy?" he started smiling.
"Can we go take a nap?" I thought about it. I was horny because I hadn't been with anybody since he was gone.
"I guess for a little while, I got something to do." Marlon had already paged me two times and every time it went off Mike would just give me a dirty look. Mike ended up making me stay until 7 pm that's when I got stern.
"Look I have to go." I called my cousin because my pager had gone off two more times and it was Marlon, and I didn't want Mike to know that I had another guy calling me.
"What up girl? I'll be through in about five minutes." I went over my cousin Shatoya's and called Marlon.
"Hey you. I left my pager at home that's why I didn't call you right back, but I can be on my way if you still want me to see me."
"You know I do. I've been waiting to see you all day." I took Marleya with me just in case Mike was following me and to make sure Marlon didn't try anything. When I walked in the door, Marlon rolled his eyes when he saw I wasn't alone. He ended up calling one of his boys over and we played cards and watched movies until around midnight, then I dropped Marleya off and went home.

CHAPTER- 20

Mike was a good manipulator and he had made his way to a good guy in my mother's eyes. All she wanted was for her baby girl to be happy and she saw that Mike was the person who made that happen.

Mike came over one Saturday afternoon and took me for some ice cream. We went to Dairy Queen. I ordered an Oreo Blizzard, and he got my mom and her boyfriend a banana split. When we returned to the house we had just walked in the door when this car flew past screeching its tires and I heard a girl yelling.

"Got damn it, that's Mike's car." We stayed in an all-white neighborhood and there was nothing around us but woods, so nobody could say *"they just drove by"* because we were out of the way. Mike heard the commotion and looked outside just in time to see Angelica and her friend at the stop sign.

"I'll be right back." Mike jogged down the stairs to his car and then I heard his tires screeching as he turned the corner. I came outside and stood on the porch. I heard people yelling, but I couldn't see anyone. "Bitch, don't be coming around here with that bull shit."

"Oh, that's how you are going to play?" Then, I couldn't hear them anymore, I thought they were making up. The next thing I know I hear a bunch of glass shatter. "Mike this isn't even my car. You are going to pay for this."

"Fuck you! I ain't paying for shit." Then I heard two car doors slam and within the next two minutes, Mike pulled back in front of my house where I was sitting on the porch. I had lost my appetite, so I had put my ice cream in the freezer, and I was ready to beat some ass. Angelica had

disrespected my mom and her house and that was something I didn't play. Mike went into the house and apologized to my mom then came back outside.
"Kya, I'm sorry, things will get better, I promise." I just looked at him dumbfounded. He kissed me on the lips.
"I'm about to go, I'll call you later." I felt my stomach do a summersault.
"Whatever." He left and I went in the house to throw up, while my stomach continued to do flips. He had proved to me that he wasn't still messing with Angelica, and he had showed her he was trying to be with me, but I still had my doubts, because that could have been a show because he knew she had to communicate with him because she was carrying his child and I had no ties. I was just going to keep my eyes open.

CHAPTER- 21

"Kya, who is that blowing up your pager?" Mike asked with a smile to make me think that he wasn't mad.
"Nothing you need to worry about." It was Damon the guy I had met at the bar.
"Well, why don't you call them back?"
"Because it's nothing." He handed me the phone and I ignored him and looked at the T.V.
"Here call them back."
"No." He snatched my pager and dialed the number and handed me the phone. I hung it back up without saying a word.
"What are you hiding?"
"I'm not hiding anything. Mike, I don't feel like playing no games with you."
"Well, I'll talk to them then." He pushed redial.
"Somebody just page Kya? Who is this? Naw nigga you paged my girl." I gave him a quick look like *what*. "Well, I'm going to tell you what, don't call her no more." He slammed the phone down. "So now you got nigga's calling you?"
"Look, you decided you were ready to move on so don't trip."
"Man, I'm not fucking with nobody, but you."
"I can't tell when you got a baby on the way."
"Man, that shit is over with, and I've been sniffing up under your ass since I got home."
"Look I'm about to go." I got up off the couch.
"You trying to run and call that nigga back?" He pushed me back down on the couch.
"I'm about to go home because you're trippin'." I got back up off the couch.

"You ain't going nowhere so sit your ass back down" and he pushed me back down on the couch. I sat there for a while, and I was getting madder and madder. After I sat there for about an hour, I guess he realized he was acting petty.
"You don't have to be here if you don't want. You can go." I did just that. I went home and went to bed. I didn't call Damon back until the next day.
"Can I speak to Damon?"
"Yeah, who is this?"
"This Kya."
"Man, who was that dude that called playing on my phone last night."
"I apologize for that."
"Is that your boyfriend?
"My ex."
"Ya'll must still be messing around."
"Naw, he just be trippin' sometimes."
"You need to handle that. Is that what my dad was talking about, that night I met you?"
"Yeah, but don't worry about it."
"Well, when can I see you?"
"Um, I got a lot of running to do today, maybe tomorrow." I really didn't have any plans, I just wasn't ready to spend time with him alone, not just yet. I needed to talk to him a few more times to see where his head was.
"Alright, well call me and let me know what's up."
"I'll do that." *He is so sweet.* I thought.
"Aye, don't be having your dudes calling my house."
"Don't worry about that."
"Alright. You stay sweet, and I'll talk to you later." As soon as I hung up the phone it rang right back.
"Hello?"

"Good morning." It was Mike.
"Hey."
"Were you sleeping?"
"Nope, I'm about to get dressed."
"What are you doing today?"
"I don't know yet."
"You want to go to the movies?"
"I don't care. What we going to see?"
"It's a couple of movies I wanted to see, so I'm going to go get a paper and I'll be over in about an hour or two."
"Alright," I got up and made some bacon, eggs and toast, got dressed and watched videos like I did every Saturday morning.

    Mike arrived at my mom's around 1 pm and I had fallen asleep on the couch. I had the front door open so I would be able to hear when Mike got there. He was so silly; he didn't knock on the door he just stood there. "Pssst." I just laid there because I thought it was the T.V. or something. "Pssst." I opened my eyes and Mike had his face on the screen. "Did I scare you?"
"No, but you are retarded." I got up and let him in.
"You ready?"
"What time the movie start?"
"1:15." I looked at my watch.
"Man, it's already 1:05."
"Well let's go."
"Let me go use the bathroom right quick." I went to relieve myself and as I was washing my hands my phone rang. I continued to get ready.
"Aren't you going to answer your phone?"
"Let the answer machine get it we already running late, or they'll call back if it's important." He just looked at me

with a mean mug on his face. I rolled my eyes and ran in my room and grabbed the phone.
"Hello."
"Hey Kya, I thought you weren't home. I was just about to leave you a message." It was Otis.
"I was on my way out the door."
"So how have you been?"
"Good, how about yourself?"
"I've been alright. Well, I'm not going to hold you I was just thinking about you and wanted to see how you were doing."
"That was nice. Thanks for calling."
"It's Okay for you to call me sometime", by this time I was cheesing from ear to ear.
"I'll do that." When I turned around Mike was standing in my doorway with his arms folded over his chest.
"I'm ready," he said with an attitude.
"Here I come."
"Who was that?"
"It was for me." I walked past him and into the hallway and he was right on my heels.
"So that nigga still calling here, huh?"
"What are you talking about?"
"Don't play dumb. Call him back."
"For what?"
"Tell him don't call you no more."
"Whatever."
Whap! He smacked me across the right side of my face. I just stood there for a minute.
I can't believe this motha fucka just hit me. I thought. I went to the hall closet, which was about two steps ahead of me, and got my stun gun out of my coat pocket and tased

him right on his side where I held it, for a good five seconds.

"Bitch!" he yelled, and he ran into the bathroom. I knew it hurt because I had accidentally stunned myself putting it into my pocket one day. I started to panic because I knew he was going to get me back some way. I ran and put the stun gun under the front of my waterbed and put my fluffy troll house shoes in front of it so he wouldn't think to look there. He stayed in the bathroom for about five minutes. He came out and went looking for my stun gun.

"Where is it?"
"What?"
"That stun gun."
"What you need it for?"
"Don't worry about it. You are going to get yours." He stormed out of the door slamming it as he exited. We never made it to the movies.

****

Shawn called me later that evening all hyped.
"Girrrrl... I'm glad you didn't go out with us tonight.
"Why, what happened?"
"You know that one dude you meet up there a couple of weeks ago?"
"Who, Damon?"
"Yeah. Mike beat his ass."
"For what?"
"I don't know, Mike was lying on the table sleep and I saw dude walk past him and the next thing I know Mike was beating his ass."
"Man, he be on some silly shit. Damon had called me last week when I was over there, and he told him not to call me anymore. Then I was over there the other night, and he

called me again and Mike recognized the number, I guess and called him back and they were arguing over the phone."
"I heard him telling his dude that Damon had kicked him when he walked past him, but I didn't see all of that. Man, that nigga crazy. Damon's mouth was all busted. His dad was pissed, but he didn't say anything because you know Andre beat his ass last week and knocked out his two front teeth.
"Man, them Southside nigga's is off the chain."
"Well, don't tell Mike I told you. See if he mentions it himself."
"Alright, I'll talk to you later."

CHAPTER- 22

"Take it off." I heard the ladies yelling as my Aunt Jazman, her friend Linda and I walked into the male revue. I went to the bar and ordered a five-dollar shot of absolute and cranberry. I gave the barmaid a twenty.
"Can I get a five and ten one's?" My aunt and Linda order their drinks and we found a table in the middle of the floor so we could still see, but there would be less of a chance that the dancer would pull us to the middle of the floor. By the time we found our seats one of the dancers had this girl on the floor with her shirt over her head, so everyone saw her breasts. She was lying on her back in the missionary position, and he was making a salad between her legs. My vagina became instantly moist. This was a new experience for me, and I liked how it was making me feel. By the third act and my second drink I was totally hot and bothered. I had never seen a butt as tight as these guys had and their bodies... oh my.
"Kya are you enjoying yourself?" asked my aunt Jazman.
"Am I? Man did you see how big that second dude's thing was?" They all started laughing. Then I felt my pager vibrating on my hip. I looked at it and it read "111". I hit the button and waited for the next act. Five minutes later my pager went off again. This time it read "111-411". I hit the button again. I only had four more dollars and the next act was about to start and brother was fine. We all got up and made our way closer to the front. I had a lot of "liquor courage" and was ready for my first dance. I started waving my dollars in the air, the dancer and I caught eyes while I was yelling "oh daddy, take it all off". He came over to me and picked me up and held me up by my butt. I wrapped my legs around his waist and my arms around his

neck and he started grinding on me, then he leaned me up against a chair. I grabbed the seat of the chair for support. The chair was behind me, and I was facing him, and he was holding onto my thighs then we started pumping and grinding real hard and I felt like I was about to bust a nut. I tried to laugh it off because I was kind of embarrassed and I didn't want anyone to see the lust in my eyes. I put two dollars in his g-string, and then he kissed me on my cheek. "Thank you, baby," and he returned to the middle of the floor. When I looked at my pager that I felt going off during my dance, I saw that Mike had paged me four times. "Aye," I got my aunts attention. "I'll be back I have to make a phone call." I went outside to the first set of doors to the pay phone and called Mike back.
"Where you at?"
"Kickin' it with my auntie, why what's up?"
"Where ya'll at?"
"We about to leave in a little bit, I'll call you when I get home."
"Bitch, I'm not playing with you. Where the fuck ya'll at?" I looked at the phone as if to say *I know he's not talking to me* then I hung it up. He paged me again about five more times and I just kept hitting the button. I went to the bar to get five more ones and my pager went off again this time it was a phone number followed by 911. Shawn was in a really bad relationship, and I tried to stay on call for her if she needed a ride and I didn't recognize the number. I went to my aunt "Aye, I'm about to go to the bathroom and see who this is that just paged me, I'll be right back." I went to the lobby with my dollars in my hand and picked up the phone and dialed the number as I was looking at my pager. It rang busy. I hung it up and when I dialed it again, I realized it was the same number that was on the pay

phone. I hung up the phone and I was a little distraught. I was walking back into the club when I felt a jerk at the collar of my shirt.
"Oh, you wanna play." I turned around and it was of Mike, and he reeked of alcohol. My heart sank to the pit of my stomach.
"Mike, what are you doing?" He just continued to drag me out of the club mumbling something under his breath.
"Get off of me!" I started trying to pull away. "Quit playing!" He never said a word. A couple of guys, one I knew from the north side, was waiting for the male revue to end, so they could come in, saw what was going on.
"Aye man, don't trip like that, they just having a good time, my girl in there too."
"Man, mind your fuckin' business." I tried to pull away, but he had such a tight grip I couldn't do anything but go along. We got to his car, and he walked me around to the passenger's seat, pushed me into the car, ran around to the other side of the car and got into the driver's seat. All I was thinking *if I could only get back into the club with my aunt, I would be safe.* As soon as the car pulled away from the curve I jumped out and hauled ass. I had on a pair of three-inch heel boots, but I ran as fast as I could. Cars were blowing their horns, but I kept running. I was about twenty-five feet from the door when I hit the ground and when I looked up Mike was pulling me up by my collar, which he had wrapped around his fist. When I got to my feet, he punched me in the mouth with the same fist he had wrapped around my shirt. "Don't try to fucking play me." He pulled me back to his car that was still running in the middle of the street. He pushed me in the driver's side and then he got in sitting on my legs. I moved over to the passenger's side, and he reached over and put my seat belt

on. I sat there and started to cry while I sucked the blood off my bottom lip.
"What the fuck are you crying for, ain't nobody hurt you?" I just kept my head down.

We arrived at his house about fifteen minutes later. I went into the bathroom to look at my face. My eyeliner had run from my crying, my lip was swollen and my top button on my shirt was hanging off. I stood in the mirror and cried as hard as I could until I felt better. When I came out of the bathroom, he was lying on the couch asleep. I sat in the chair on the other side of the room. I couldn't leave because he had the keys to the door, and I didn't have a way to get anywhere. I picked up the phone to call my aunt's boyfriend so if she called or came home, she would know where I was.
"Who are you calling?" he jumped up from the couch and grabbed the phone.
"My aunt is probably looking for me. I need to let her know I'm ok."
"What's the number? I'll dial it."
"I don't know I need to call her boyfriend and get the number." He gave me the phone. I dialed her home phone, but no one answered.
"She's going to call the police, because she's going to think I got kidnapped." I looked at my watch and it was only 10:48 and the male revue wasn't over until midnight, so she wasn't going to look for me for a while.
"Can you make me some soup?" I just sat there thinking *I know he's not talking to me.* He ran into the bathroom and threw up. I ignored him and kept sitting there. He walked out of the bathroom holding his stomach. "Kya, can you please make me some soup?" I went into the kitchen and

opened a can of chicken noodle soup, poured it into a bowl and put it into the microwave. When it beeped, I sat the bowl on the table by the couch where he was lying. He just continued to lie there until the doorbell rang. He looked out of the window and went outside on the porch and closed the house door. I heard a female voice, so I looked out of the window, and it was Cheryl. I guess that's who he was with all day, because I had paged him about seven times earlier and he had never called me back. "I thought you were coming back." I heard Cheryl say. She didn't know I was in there because my car wasn't outside. I was mad as hell. *How the fuck this nigga going to be with his bitch all day and then try to check me.* I went over and spit in his soup as I tried to hold back my tears, but they just started flowing down my face. He came back in about five minutes later and warmed up his soup again and ate it. Around 11:45 he took me back to the club and all the men were lined up waiting to go inside. The guy working the door remembered me from the episode earlier that evening and he just let me walk past.

"Are you alright?" I just shook my head yes and continued to walk back into the club. I spotted my aunt right away. "Where have you been? I checked the bathroom and everywhere." I looked at her and I broke down crying. She laid my head on her shoulder and patted my back. "I'm going to fuck that nigga up." She already knew. She brought me another drink and I told her all about what happened on the ride back to her house. When we got to her house I didn't go inside, I got into my car and drove home. When I arrived at my house I parked my car behind the house, so if Mike was to drive by, he would think I wasn't home. I turned the ringer off on my house phone and I turned my pager off. I didn't want to hear Mike's voice. I was tired of him hurting me and trying to run my life, but I didn't know what to do.

****

Wednesday morning, I left for work early, so if Mike called or came over, I wouldn't be there, and I didn't show up for his bowling practice that I went to every Wednesday. I kept my ringer off on my phone, my pager stayed off and I put my car back behind the house, so he would still think I wasn't home. The next afternoon Mike called me at work.
"Hey Kya. What are you doing?"
"About to go to lunch."
"Well come on, I'm outside." I took a deep breath and walked slowly down to the gate. I hesitantly got into the car, and he kissed me like nothing had happened. We went to McDonald's and then to the Lake. We walked around the lake, fed the ducks and he taught me how to skip rocks in the water as we talked. "Kya, I'm sorry about the other night. When ya'll going out again?" I just looked at him distraught. He started smiling. "I was going to give you some money, since I messed up your evening."
"They only have them on the first Tuesday of every month so..." I shrugged my shoulders.
We walked around the lake one more time, and then it was time for me to go back to work. He let me out at the gate closest to my building.
"When you get off work today come by. I got something for you."

When I got to Mike's Angelica was picking up their son. Mike had called me a few weeks prior and told me he

was at the hospital, and she was having the baby, so I knew he was trying to be open and show me he was doing right. I sat down in the chair to let her know I wasn't going anywhere anytime soon. After about five minutes I guess she got a clue and got their things together and they left. Mike came out of the kitchen and sat on the arm of the chair that I was sitting in.
"Are you hungry?"
"A little bit."
"I made some steak. Are you staying for dinner?"
"Why not?" He made us a salad with cucumbers and tomatoes and Italian salad dressing. We ate dinner and we both fell asleep on the couch. I woke up about 6:30 pm. I shook him to wake him up.
 "Mike, I have to go." I got up from the couch.
 "Hold up, I got something for you. Come here." He pulled me down on his lap, so I was facing him and he took a ring off of his necklace.
"Can you fit that?" It was another dollar sign ring except it was smaller than the first one he had given me. It fit perfectly on my pinky finger.
"Yup."
"You can have it."
"Thank you." I went home and spent some time with my mom.

CHAPTER- 23

"Come on Kya, get up. Let's go down to the Treetop and have us a drink." It was 10:30pm and Mike and I had tried to sleep the day away.
"I don't want to wear this, let me go home and change."
"Man, you look fine, just fix your hair and let's go." Mike called his brother, while I was getting myself together. We got to the Treetop, and everyone was showing Mike much love like they always did. He brought me an absolute and cranberry and every time my glass was halfway full one of his boys would replenish my drink. Mike was not the kind of guy that took a girl to the bar, so his boys figured it must be something special. One of the guys came over to the table where I was sitting and sat a bottle of champagne on the table. No one ever said anything to me they just handed me a glass. Mike came over to the table and popped the cork off the champagne bottle and poured me, his brother, one of his boys, and himself a glass.
"Here's a toast to me and my baby", and he kissed me on the lips. We all hit our glasses together and took a sip of our drinks. By the end of the night I had, had six glasses of absolute and cranberry and they were not shots, they were in Kool-Aid glasses, and we finished off the bottle of champagne. I was still working on my sixth drink, and I just kept looking at my glass and the more I drank it seemed like the fuller the glass would get. I was trying to finish my drink, but I couldn't. I could no longer feel my fingers; it felt like my whole body was numb. The next thing I know Mike's brother Kevin was shaking my shoulder.
"Get up! You don't do that in here!" I had fallen asleep in a chair. I looked around and it felt like the whole room was

spinning. I spotted Mike he was in front of me playing darts.
"Mike." I got up and tapped him on the shoulder.
"What's the matter baby?"
"I'm ready to go."
"Here I come." He handed his boy his darts and asked him to finish his game because he could tell I wasn't with it. We get outside to the car, and I hand him the keys.
"I'm not driving. Man, I'm fucked up."
"Me too and you're use to driving while you're drunk", and I got in on the passenger's side.
"Man, you're trippin'." We drove back to his house, and we went inside. He went to use the bathroom while I lied down on the couch.
"Come on Kya." I opened one eye and looked at him like he was crazy. It was one o'clock in the morning.
"Where are we going? Man, I'm tired."
"Let's go get a room."
"For what?" It's late we might as well stay here."
"I don't want to be here."
"Man, that's just a waist of money."
"Why, you always gotta make things so difficult?"
"You know what? And I started getting up from the couch.
"We don't have to get a room; I'll just go home. You just don't want your ugly ass baby mama to come over here and see me here." I started walking towards the door.
"What did you say?"
"You heard me."
"Who are you talking about?" He squinted his eyes and stuck his neck out.
"Cheryl's ugly ass. He started walking towards me real fast. "Now give me my keys so I can leave."

WHAPP!! He smacked me in the mouth so hard I fell against the door.
"I know you didn't just hit me because of that bitch."
"Shut the fuck up!"
"I don't have to; this is my mouth." He smacked me again and I staggered backwards. I caught my balance, balled up my fist and punched him in the mouth as hard as I could. He grabbed me with both of his hands by the collar of my shirt and threw me over the couch. As I was getting up, he jumped over the arm of the couch and landed on top of me and started punching me in my head and face. I put my arms up to block my face and I started squirming around on the couch until I scooted down between his legs so he couldn't hit me anymore and I could get up. He started getting up from the couch because he was in an awkward position. He had his right foot on the floor and his left knee was still on the couch. I moved my hands from my face to wipe the blood I tasted in my mouth, and he smacked me again. My legs were now free so I kicked him in his nuts as hard as I could. He grabbed himself and rolled off the couch. I got up and ran out of the front door.
"Fuck!" I yelled. Then I remembered seeing the keys lying on the living room table. I ran back into the house and grabbed the keys from the table and Mike started getting up. I was fumbling through the keys trying to find the key when Mike came on the porch and smacked the keys out of my hands, and they fell on the porch. He dragged me back into the house. I grabbed a hold of the doorframe, but he was pulling me so hard all my fingers did were slip off. He closed the door, and I took off running toward the bathroom and he caught me in the dining room. He pushed me up against his built-in shelf that separated the kitchen and the dinning room, where he kept his trophies. All the

trophies on the lower shelf fell to the floor. I tried to run around him, but he had me in the corner. I reached around him to grab one of the trophies to hit him with, but he smacked my hand down. I looked around and there was nothing I could do. I looked in his eyes and there was hate and I knew this was not over. I balled up my fists and hit him with a right left combination. He staggered back and punched me on the left side of my face. I swung back, but I missed, and he came back with another right that caught me on the right side of my face. I swung again and hit him in the mouth. He picked up his dining room chair, which was leather with a metal bottom with four wheels and hit me in the face and I fell to the ground. He proceeded to kick me in the face, the stomach and everywhere else that he could. I curled up in a fetal position to protect my face. *This nigga is about to kill me,* I thought. I knew I had to think quickly. I grabbed my stomach.
"Mike the baby." I knew Mike wanted us to have a baby that was his dream; he already had a name for it and everything.
"What you say?"
"Mike, I was going to tell you when the time was right. I'm pregnant." He just stood there and started crying. I got up and wiped the warm liquid I felt running down my face. I looked at my hand and it was covered with blood. I lost it.
"What the fuck you do to me?" I ran in the bathroom and looked in the mirror. My right eye was swollen, my nose and mouth were bleeding and blood was gushing out of my forehead where he had hit me with the chair. I started crying like a baby. It was dark in the dining room, so Mike hadn't seen the damage he had done. He came into the bathroom and saw my face and he panicked. His eyes got big, and he ran into the kitchen, got a rag out of the dryer,

put some ice in it and came back into the bathroom. He wiped the blood from my face and put the ice on my forehead.
"Get off of me." I pushed him away from me and went into the living room and picked up the phone to call my mom. He snatched the phone out of the wall.
"Who are you calling?"
"My mom."
"For what?" I started crying again. "I want my mommy." He held me in his arms.
"Come on let's go."
"Where are we going?"
"Just come on."
"Are you taking me to the hospital?"
"Come on." I got up still crying and we went outside, and I started crying even louder hoping to get the attention of some of his neighbors. We got into my car, since he still had my keys and we drove off. I closed my eyes and leaned back on the seat because my head was killing me.

   I opened my eyes when I felt the car stop. I looked around and we were at a motel. I couldn't see the name of it because he had pulled around to the side. I laid my head back down when he looked my way to act like I was asleep. He got out of the car and took the keys and turned on the alarm so he would know if I got out of the car. When he went into the building to get our room I reached into my purse and got out my cell phone I had just brought the day before and called my dad to come to my rescue.
"Cleo." I never called my dad, dad.
"Kya?"
"Yeah."
"What's wrong?"

"Mike hit me in the face with a metal chair and he busted my head, my eye is swollen, and my lip is busted."
"Where you at?"
"I don't know at some motel. I can't see a sign."
"Alarm deactivated", I heard my car say and I looked over and Mike was putting the key into the door. My windows were tinted, and it was dark so Mike couldn't see that I was on the phone.
"I gotta go, here he come." I was trying to ease my phone back into my purse and it fell onto the floor.
"Who were you talking to?"
"Shawn."
"Oh. Come on." We went inside the room, and it was beautiful, it had a heart shaped Jacuzzi and everything, but too bad I couldn't enjoy it. He made me keep ice on my eye and my forehead for the rest of the night. We checked out at 10:00 am the next day. I looked in the mirror when I got into the car, and I had a black eye and a big gash with two knots on my forehead. My lip was swollen only a little, but the inside was cut badly. I looked a total mess and Mike was going to pay for this.

    Mike drove back to his house and parked in front of the door. I got out and walked around to the driver's seat, while he was getting out leaving the car running. I got into the car, and he stood in front of the door so that I couldn't shut it. He just stared at me, but I wouldn't look him in the eyes.
"Baby I'm so sorry." I shook my head yes, and that made my splinting headache worst. "I love you so much Kya." He bent down to kiss me, and I moved away from him and turned up my nose. He looked at me with tears in his eyes.

"I'm sorry baby" and a tear rolled down his face. "Tell your mom that we went out and you got jumped."
"I'm not lying for you. Mike it's over. Please don't call me anymore", and I started closing the door and he moved out of the way so that I could. He walked over to get into his car and watched me until my car disappeared.

When I got home, I went in the house and was walking towards my bedroom.
"Kya", my mom called from the living room. I stopped in the hallway, never turning around. "Come here." My dad had already informed her about what was going on and from the looks of her eyes and her ashtray; she had been up all-night crying and smoking cigarettes. I sat on the couch across the room from where she was sitting. She looked at my face.
"Mike did that to you?" I shook my head yes and my eyes filled up with tears. "Okay, go ahead and go in your room." I went into my room and lay across the bed. I heard my mom talking, but I couldn't make out what she was saying. I had dozed off and woke up to someone banging on the door. I heard the door open and then shut. "Kya, come here." I went into the living room and there were two uniformed police officers standing by the door. "See what he did to her?" The female officer looked at my face and shook her head. "I want him prosecuted to the fullest." The other officer took out a notebook and an ink pen from his shirt pocket.
"Okay ma'am, tell me what happened." I looked at him, but I never said a word.
"Kya, tell them what happened." I looked at my mom and then at the police officers and then I dropped my head and looked at the floor.

"Ma'am, we need your statement in order to prosecute him." I still didn't say anything, tears just rolled down my cheeks.
"I'll give the statement. Kya you can go back to your room." I went back to my room just as my dad was pulling up.
"How old is she?"
"She's nineteen."
"Well unfortunately, she's considered an adult and you can't give a statement for her. We need her testimony in order to pursue this."
"Look at her face. You can't go off that?"
"I'm sorry ma'am we can't. I know you're looking out for the best interest of your daughter, but she needs to come forward."
"Cleo, talk to your daughter, she is sitting in there looking like Cyclops and she won't tell them what happened." My dad came into my room and sat on the side of my bed.
"What's up?" I shook my head side to side.
"Why don't you tell them what happened?"
"I want him to pay, but I don't want to see him locked up again."
"What do you want to see happen to him?" I shrugged my shoulders. He sat there in silence for a few minutes then he went back into the living room with my mom and closed my door behind him. I heard the officers leave, then a few minutes later my parents left too.

My mom and dad both met up unexpectedly at Mike's house. My mom with her gun and my dad with a baseball bat, but Mike wasn't home. My mom went to one end of the street and my dad to the other waiting patiently for Mike to return. They waited for two hours, but he never came home.

CHAPTER- 24

Beep, Beep, Beep. I looked at my pager and it read "143", which meant I love you. I knew it was from Mike because that was our thing. I hit the button and finished my math test. I t was a good thing I had long hair. I had cut my bangs short so that I could cover up my lumpy forehead and I wore the right side down over my eye. The bruises weren't totally covered, but they weren't as obvious. Mike called me everyday and told me that he loved me, and I would just say okay and hang up.

The following Monday, Mike had his daughter Divine call me, he knew that was like my daughter and I wouldn't be mean to her.
"Hi Kya."
"Hi. Who is this?"
"This is Divine."
"Oh, how are you doing?"
"Fine. My daddy said he love you."
"Tell him, okay."
"Why don't you come over no more?"
"I'm usually at school or at work all the time."
"Oh. Can you come over Saturday so we can go to the movies?"
"I'll see."
"Okay."
"Well, I have to go; I'll talk to you later."
"Okay. Wait my daddy wants you." Mike got on the phone.
"That was real low Mike."
"What?"
"To use the kids, come on."

"I just wanted to hear your voice. I miss you Kya and so does the kids."
"Whatever Mike, didn't you see what you did to my face?"
"Yes, I did and I'm sorry, baby you'll never have to worry about that again."
"I know."
"Why don't you come over here tomorrow when you get off work? I need to talk to you."
"You're already talking to me."
"No, I want a face-to-face conversation."
"I don't know Mike. You have really out done yourself this time."
"Please. I promise you don't ever have to worry about that again. I was wrong. I don't know what came over me."
"Just call me tomorrow."
"Okay baby, I love you." Then Divine got back on the phone.
"Kya?"
"What's up baby?"
"I love you."
"Okay, I'll talk to ya'll later. I was so confused, I still loved Mike and I enjoyed his kids. We had been through so much together and I didn't want what we had to end like this.

    I went over Mike's after I got out of class that evening. I walked into the living room and sat on the couch.
"So, what you want to talk about?"
"Us."
"Okay."
"I know that you've been on me about getting a job for the past year or so, and I've done that. I'm opening a car wash,

with a mechanic in the back and I'm opening a corner store with a game room on the other side. I've been saving my money to do the right thing with."
"That's good. I'm glad you're trying to better yourself."
"That's not all." I started fiddling with my fingers. "Stefanie is coming to stay with me for a while." Stefanie was another one of Mike's daughters. She was ten years old and just as cute as she wanted to be. She reminded me of a china doll. She and I had really bonded to the point that every time she came to visit her dad, she would have him call me. Even though I didn't have any kids, she would come over and we'd play board games or go walk around the mall, or I'd stay over Mike's house until she went home. She was like the daughter I never had.
"That's good."
"So, you know she's going to want to be up under you." That brought a smile to my face because I knew he was telling the truth and that was my girl. "And one more thing." Mike got up and ran up the stairs while I sat on the couch waiting for him to return. He came back downstairs and sat on the couch beside me. I gave him a confused look because he didn't have anything in his hand. He continued to stare at me smiling.
"What?"
"I love you Kya, and we are going have us a pretty baby", and he rubbed my stomach. I pushed his hand off me.
"There is no baby." His eyes got big, and he continued to stare at me.
"You killed my baby?" I shook my head no. He looked in my eyes trying to see if I was lying. I cut my eyes to break our stare. I loved kids too much and I would never have an abortion. He didn't believe me, and I didn't care. I wanted him to think I killed his baby because I wanted him to hurt

like I had. I know my absence had hurt him, but that wasn't enough. He got up from the couch and knelt down between my legs, and then he kissed me on the lips.
"Kya, I love you so much and I want us to be a family." He went into the pocket of his hoodie and pulled out a one-karat diamond ring and put it on my finger. My eyes got big because this was what I wanted, but I had made up my mind, I was through with him and I knew my parents wouldn't approve, after what he had just done to me.
"Mike, I can't accept this", and I went to pull the ring from my finger. He grabbed both of my hands.
"Yes, you can baby, we're going to work this out and be a happy family. I've done everything you've been asking me to do for the past two years and I'm a better man and I want a chance to show you." I sat there and thought about it for a minute.
"Okay Mike, but we're not going to rush into anything. We're going to take this slow and if you ever hit me again I …" He cut me off.
"Baby you don't have to worry about that."
"Okay we'll see. Well, I have to go because I don't want my mom to be worried about me."
"Okay baby. Call me later."

      That following week I went to Colorado to clear my head. I also wanted to see my new niece and spend some time with my older brother Cleo, who was back from Desert Storm. When I returned a week later Mike, and I were inseparable. Every time I took a step, he was right there behind me. He showed me so much love for the next two years that I knew that this was the guy I was going spend to rest of my life with and not once did he raise his hands to me. He pushed me a couple of times, but he never hit me and at the time I didn't realize that that was a form of abuse. We had our disagreements like all couples do, but we would talk out our differences.

CHAPTER- 25

Mike had given me some money so that I could get my hair done. When I was finished, I went back to Mike's house. I was in the living room watching T.V. when Mike's house phone rang.
"Hello?"
"Can I speak to Mike please?"
"Yeah, hold on a second." I had been answering Mike's phone for the past two years and he never had a problem with it. I went to the door.
"Mike." He looked my way. "Phone."
"Who is it?
"Angelica." He came into the house, and they talked for a minute and then he went back on the porch. About five minutes later the phone rang again. This time it was Cheryl. When she heard my voice, she smacked her lips.
"Where's Mike?" I put the phone down and went back to the door.
"Mike, phone again."
"Man, who is it?"
"Cheryl."
"Tell her I will call her back." I went back to the phone with a big smile on my face.
"He said he'd call you back."
"What?" I hung the phone up. The phone rang right back, and it was Angelica again.
"Mike Angelica is on the phone again."
"Man, you talk to her, you keep answering the phone." I laid the phone on the couch thinking Mike was just playing. He came in the house a couple of minutes later and walked past the phone and went into the bathroom.

"*If you'd like to make a call, please hang up and try your call again*", the operator said. Angelica had hung up. I hung up the phone and headed toward the bathroom to see what was wrong with Mike when I heard him talking. I stood outside the bathroom door for a second then I went in. When I opened the door Mike looked up at me real fast and he had this guilty look on his face. I could hear a girl's voice, but it was kind of muffled and I couldn't make out whom it was. I stood in the doorway with my arms folded over my chest until he ended his call.
"What?" he asked.
"What's wrong with you?" I walked over to the mirror and started fixing my hair.
"What I tell you about putting that fake shit in your hair?" I had my hair finger waved in the front and set curled in the back with four two-inch tracks sporadically in my set so it would look like my hair was streaked blue.
"That's what you have an attitude about?"
"No, but I don't like that fake shit." He went into the kitchen and came back into the bathroom and poured a cup of water over my head. I grabbed my washcloth from the towel bar and wiped the gel that was running down my face from my finger waves.
"You play too much" and I hit him with my rag. He pushed me up against the sink.
"I'm about to go", and I started walking towards the bathroom door.
"You ain't goin' nowhere" and he pulled me back into the bathroom. He picked me up and threw me onto the floor. I started kicking at him.
"Get off of me!" Tommy heard the commotion and ran into the bathroom and pulled Mike by his shirt.

"Mike, get off her. Man, it's not worth it." I got up and started walking out of the door. He pushed me from behind and I fell on the ground. I got up and pushed him back and he fell into the door.

"Whap!" He took his hand all the back to yesterday and smacked the shit out of me. I grabbed my face and tears started rolling down my cheek. I took off my one-karat ring and threw it at him.

"I told you if you ever hit me again I was out, and I meant that shit." I started walking towards my car that was parked on the street. He picked up the ring and ran behind me.

"You ain't going nowhere. You my woman." I was trying to hurry up and get the key in the door, but my hands were shaking too badly. He pushed me and my keys fell to the ground.

"Mike why are you doing this?" and I picked up my keys and started slowly walking around to the other side of the car. "You know I love you; I don't know why you're treating me like this?" I found the key and leaned my body over the top of the car. "I want this to work, but you can't keep putting your hands on me." I stuck the key into the passenger door while I was still leaning on the top of the car talking to Mike.

"I'm sorry baby. Here, take your ring back." Mike was still in the street on the driver's side of the car. I stood up to act like I was going to reach for the ring then I opened the passenger door, got into the car and locked the door. Mike tried to open the driver's door, but it was still locked. He ran around to the other side of the car while I jumped over the console and into the driver's seat, and he tried to open that door, but it was locked too. I put the key into the ignition, and he kicked my window. I started the car up and he ran in front of the car and put his hands on the hood and stood there. I put the car in drive and mashed on the gas. Mike went up in the air and landed on the hood of the car. He rolled off the side of the car and fell to the ground. I pressed on the gas harder and my car bounced up on the right side, and I knew I had run over something.

"Ahhhhh," I heard Mike yell, but I kept going. I looked in my rear-view mirror just as Mike was throwing a brick at my car, but I was too far away for him to hit me. When I got to the top of the hill about eight blocks away, I called my dad.

"Aye, I'm about to come over."

"What's wrong?" It was 11:30 pm and I never called my dad that late.

"Mike and I got into it again, but he didn't hurt me, but I think I hurt him."

"Good. Did you kill him?"

"No." And I started laughing.

"Shoot."

"But I did run him over, I felt the car go bloop, bloop, and then he started screaming."

"All man, is he hurt?"

"I don't know. I didn't stick around to see. But I know he's going to come to my mom's house looking for me and I don't want him upsetting her or doing anything to my car. He won't look for me over your house."

"Alright, I'll let you in the garage." I went to my dad's, and we talked until one in the morning. Then he gave me a blanket and I fell asleep on the couch.

CHAPTER- 26

I woke up Saturday morning around 8:30. I sat up and rubbed my neck because it was sore from sleeping on the arm of my dad's couch. I looked at my pager that was lying on the floor on vibrate and I had three missed pages. They all read "111-911-911". I cleared my pages and got my cell phone from the love seat, and I had seven missed calls, which I assumed were from Mike too. I went down the hall and knocked on my dad's bedroom door.
"Yeah."
"I'm about to go."
"Wait a minute, here I come." I went into the kitchen, and he came out of his room.
"Are you going to be alright?"
"Yeah, I'm about to go home."
"Well, you call me as soon as you get in the door."
"I will," and I went home. My dad only lived about five minutes from me, so I got there pretty quickly.

As I was walking through the door, I heard my phone ringing. I ran up the stairs, but by the time I got my bedroom door unlocked the answering machine had already picked it up and whomever it was hung up. I walked into my room, and I had four messages. I pressed the play button, and the first call was a hang up call, so I pressed delete. "Hey Kya", when I heard Mike's voice I pressed delete. "Kya, I'm sorry I..." I pressed delete again and the last call was also a hang up call. I called my dad to let him know I had made it home safely and then I went into the kitchen to make some bacon, eggs and toast when my mom's phone rang.

"Hello?" *Everyone knows she's at work, who could be calling her?* I thought.
"Oh, so you can't answer your phone or return none of my calls, huh?"
"Mike, what do you want?"
"You owe me an apology."
"For what?"
"My hand is swollen like a big marshmallow. I can't even make a fist and I can't put any pressure on my foot. I've been taking pain pills all night." He sounded so pitiful; I started feeling kind of sorry for him.
"Why don't you go to the hospital?"
"I wanted to see if these pills would work first. Why don't you come take me?"
"I don't think so."
"See you don't care about me."
"That's the problem, I care too much. It's like the more I give you the more you hurt me, and Mike, I'm tired. I'm a good woman and I deserve better."
"You are a good woman, that's way I love you so much."
"If you love me than why do you do me like you do? You wouldn't hit your mama and you promised me that you would never hit me again."
"I didn't hit you. You fucked me up." I started laughing.
"It's not funny. You got me good man, we even. Well let me call my cousin and see if he'll take me to the hospital."
"Alright."
"I love you Kya."
"I love you too." *Mike didn't really hurt me this time and I did get him good. I'm lost without him. I'll give him one more chance. They say three strikes and you're out. He's on strike number two.* I thought.

I went over Mike's that evening to check on him.
He had his arm in a splint because his hand was sprained,
his foot was bandaged up and he had crutches because his
foot was fractured. Mike was lying on the couch asleep
when I got there. Tommy let me in, and I sat on the couch.
I picked up the medicine bottle that was lying on the table,
800 milligrams; I could see why he was asleep. I sat there
for a couple of hours to make sure he didn't need anything
and then I went back home.

CHAPTER- 27

"What's up Kya, the girls and me are going to the Male Revue tonight to celebrate my birthday. Are you coming?" asked Wilma.
"Yeah, I'll meet ya'll there. What time is ya'll going?"
"About nine."
"Alright, I'll see you there." I arrived at the Male Revue at 9:15 and it was packed as usual. We left there about 2:30 am, because we stayed until they closed. I went over Mike's because I was in the mood. I pulled in front of his house and his car wasn't in the driveway. I got out and knocked on the door anyway and no one answered. I paged him with "111-411" meaning what's up, and then I went home. I called his cell phone, but I got his voicemail. I paged him again with "111-911-911", saying it was an emergency, and I fell asleep waiting for him to call me back. I woke up the next morning around 6:45 and I called him again and I still got his voicemail. I paged him with a "111-335-335", which meant see what I'm talking about. Mike called me at work at 11:30 am.
"Where have you been?"
"Sleep..."
"I came by your house, and you weren't there."
"I was handling some business and then I fell asleep at the spot."
"Whatever. Well, I can't talk; I have to finish this report."
"Well call me when you get home." Instead of calling Mike I went over his house because classes were canceled, but he didn't know that. I knocked on the door and he let me in. I walked in the living room and Angelica was sitting on the couch with their son. I rolled my eyes and sat down in the chair while Mike went into the kitchen. We all sat in

the living room for about an hour looking stupid, nobody saying a word. Angelica finally got up and left and about ten minutes later I did too.

    Mike and I had planned to go the movies that Saturday afternoon. I called him about 11:30 that morning and he wasn't home. I paged him and went into the living room to watch TV while I waited for him to either call me back or come pick me up. I paged him about ten times and at 8:00 pm he pulled in front of the house. I was pissed and couldn't wait to hear this excuse. He walked on the porch like nothing was wrong.
"Where you been all day?"
"Working…"
"I went down to the car wash and to the store and you weren't there."
"You must have just missed me."
"Well why didn't you call me back or answer your cell phone?"
"I just told you I was working, now you ready or what?" I already had my shoes on because I had, had them on all day. I went to the car and sat there with an attitude. We went to the movies and then to dinner and I stayed the night over his house. We were lying on the couch asleep when I heard his pager vibrating on the floor. He didn't move and then it went off again. I rolled over and picked his pager up from the floor and looked at his new calls and they both read "22-22." That was Angelica's code. I looked at the clock and it read 2:16 am. I figured she must have been calling about their baby, so I just set the pager back on the floor.

Sunday morning Mike was in the kitchen making us breakfast when the light on his phone lit up, which meant he had his ringer off, and he didn't want to be bothered. I looked at the caller ID and it was Angelica. I ate my breakfast and went home and called Angelica back. I dialed the number, and a female answered the phone.
"Angelica?"
"Yes."
"Hey, this is Kya."
"Okay."
"No, disrespect, but I want to know why do you keep calling Mike in the middle of the night?"
"You need to grow up. We do have a child together."
"Well, the only time you need to call him is when it's concerning your child."
"Whatever."
"And I know you're the one that slashed my tire."
"Yes, I did, and I apologize. Didn't Mike get it fixed?"
"Yes, he did but that's beside the point."
"I said I was sorry."
"Yeah, because I was going to beat your ass about that, but it's cool."
"How did you get my phone number?"
"From Mike…"
"Does he know that you're calling me?"
"I don't know."
"Well, I'll be sure to let him know."
"That's fine with me."
"So, I take it you're still messing with Mike."
"Ahh, yeah…"
"Well, we're trying to work out our differences so we can raise our son right."
"Is that so?"

"It sure is."
"Okay, we'll see about that" and we ended our call. Mike called me five minutes later.
"Why the fuck are you calling playing on Angelica's phone?"
"Why the fuck are you calling here trying to check me when ya'll suppose to be working out your differences for your son's sake." I said mimicking her.
"What?"
"That's what she said."
"Man, she just fuckin' with your head."
"Yeah, time will tell."
"Whatever and you better forget that number just as easy as you got it." I hung up the phone.

    For the next month there had been weird numbers coming across Mike's pager. If I were around, I would call them back and ask, "did someone call Mike?" and they would hang up on me. I confronted Mike with it.
"Who is this bitch that keeps paging you?"
"Who?"
"I don't know who she is, but here's her number" and I read the number to him.
"Somebody keeps playing on my pager."
"Well, you need to handle that shit." Mike had come over one Thursday evening.
"Kya, we need to talk", and he was carrying a bag of Chinese food in his hand. We went downstairs into the dining room so my mother couldn't hear our conversation.
"What's wrong?" He took a deep breath.
"I got really drunk one night and I met this girl at the bar, and I went to her house and..." he paused and looked up at me.

"And what?"
"Well, you need to go down to the clinic and get checked out."
"What?"
"They gave me some pills."
"That bitch burned you. You didn't have enough respect for me to strap the fuck up if you were going to cheat."
"It was stupid and I'm sorry, but at least I was a man about it. I came and told you."
"Alright, I'm not even going to trip." Then his pager went off. He looked at it and then he looked up at me. I got up and went upstairs to the living room and got the cordless phone and handed it to him.
"Here call them back." He shook his head as he dialed the number, the same number that I'd been trying, but they kept hanging up on me.
"Why the fuck do you keep calling me playing on my pager? I told you I got a woman, so stop calling." I took the phone from him and put it to my ear.
"Oh, so that's how it is Mike?" she asked.
"Why the fuck do you keep calling my man?"
"I want him to take me to get something to eat."
"Well, he's not and now I've heard him tell you not to call him anymore, so if I see your number come across his pager again, I'm going to be to see you."
"You can come now. Mike knows where I live down on North Street."
"A project bitch... I should have known."
"Don't get mad because I got your man."
"Girl please, you may have had him, but you don't got him" and I hung up the phone.
"Come on Mike let's go."
"Where are we going?"

"On North Street to see this bitch."
"For what?"
"I need to let off some frustration."
"Man", he waved his hand at me. "She ain't even worth it."
I stood there with my hands on my hips and stared at him.
"You know what, you're right. I need to be dealing with your ass. They say every dog has its day" and in my mind I started plotting.
"What you mean by that? Man, don't start tripping."
"I'm not." We ate our Chinese food and Mike left.

    I called Mike Friday morning on my way to work.
"What are you doing?"
"Sleeping..."
"What you had a late night?"
"No, I couldn't sleep."
"Oh, do you have any plans for this evening?"
"No. Why what's up?"
"I wanted you to come over and have dinner with me."
"For real. What time?"
"About seven. Let me make my way down to the clinic and see what's up and then I'll start cooking when I get home."
"I'll be there."
"Okay, don't be late."
"I won't baby." I went down to the clinic when I got off work and sure enough, he had got me, but I had already prepared myself the night before for my revenge. I took some Italian salad dressing and put it in a zip lock bag and poured some Ammonia in it and let it sit over night. When I got up the next morning, I smelt it to see if the Ammonia scent was still overpowering the Italian dressing and it was, so I put a little vinegar in it to kill the smell and let it sit

until I came home that evening. I put in my Chocolate City CD and skipped the tracks until I found *"a thin line"* and I put it on repeat. *That mutha fucka is going to learn I'm the wrong one to fuck with. I have been nothing but good to his ass and he just keeps fucking me around and he's going to pay for this one.* I thought to myself.

I sang along with the song until my steak and baked potatoes were done, *"it's a thin line between love and hate."* I turned off my CD player and set the table with candles and champagne glasses. Mike arrived about 6:45. I greeted him at the door with a kiss.

"Uh, something smells good." He went into the bathroom and came back into the kitchen where I was making our plates.

"You need some help?"

"You can put some ice in the glasses and pour the champagne. He went downstairs and did that while I continued to prepare our plates. I made his salad, poured the Italian dressing out of the zip lock bag, onto his salad and took him his food all at once. I made sure I gave him extra tomatoes and cucumbers because they were his favorite. I took my food down and sat at the other end of the table and blessed our food. Mike was eating his salad and he looked up at me with a distraught look. I smiled at him.

"Are you enjoying your meal?" I asked him in calm voice.

"It's alright." We finished our food.

"I hope you enjoyed that because that's the last meal you'll ever get from me."

"What are you trying to say?" He grabbed a hold of his stomach and ran upstairs to throw up. "Man, I don't feel good. Did you poison me?"

"Do you think I would do something like that to you?" and I smiled at him.
"Man, I'm about to go home. I don't feel good" and he threw up again when he got outside. Mike was sick for three days. Every time he tried to eat something he would throw up and he was using the bathroom every half an hour. I called to make sure he was still alive, but I never went to see him. I wasn't trying to kill him, but I wanted him to know that I would.

CHAPTER- 28

The next three months didn't change much, every time I called Mike, he wasn't home and when I paged him it usually took him three or four hours to call me back. I'd go by his house at two and three in the morning and he was never home. Every time we had an engagement, most of the time he reneged or never showed up. I rode past Angelica's house a couple of times and saw his car parked outside and when I asked him about it "something was wrong with his son or he was just checking up on them", it was always an excuse. After a while it got old, and I was fed up. I called my brother Cleo who had moved to Georgia.

"Hey Trina," Trina was Cleo's wife. "How are you doing?"
"Good, how about yourself?"
"It could be better. How is my fat niece?"
"My little Tatar tot is good and chunky, looking just like ya'll. I didn't have anything to do with her all I did was push her out." We started laughing.
"So is Cleo around?"
"Yeah, hold on a minute." Cleo came to the phone.
"What's up?"
"Nothing, trying to get away from here."
"Why, what's wrong?"
"Nothing, I just need a break. I'm tired of Mike, but I just can't seem to let go."
"You're in love."
"I know, but I need to get away."
"Well, you can come down here for a while."
"I go on spring break in two weeks, so let me call the airlines and get my tickets and I'll let you know what time to pick me up from the airport."

"Alright, I'll see you in a couple of weeks."

    I arrived in Georgia, and it was a real change in weather. I had on a pair of jeans and a sweatshirt, and it had to be at least 80 degrees outside. The airport was about an hour drive back to Cleo's house so that gave Trina and me plenty of time to caught up on the girl talk, since she and my niece Quantas who we called Taytay came to pick me up. Cleo was still working, and Trina was still in the Military, so I spent most of my time at the house with Taytay. I did get a chance to meet some of Cleo's fine friends, but I already knew they were off limits. My brother wouldn't dare allow me to mess with any of his friends; he had made that clear with them and me. I went to the malls and the outlets and got some real nice gear that nobody had in Ohio.

    Trina had brought a whole lot of liquor for us to kick it with and every time I put a drink to my mouth, or I smelt the liquor I got nauseated. I was a drinker, and I didn't understand what the problem was.
"Dang Trina, this Apple Boon's is good, but I can't drink it. It's making me sick."
"Are you pregnant?"
"No, I just had my period before I came down here."
"That doesn't mean anything; it could have been your last one." After three of four days, I was really missing Mike and I just wanted to hear his voice. I knew he should have been at work, so I called him at the car wash and some girl answered the phone.
"Who is this?"
"This is Maureen, who is this?"

"This is Mike's woman and why are you answering the phone?"
"I work here."
"Where is Mike?" She smacked her lips.
"Hold on." Mike came to the phone breathing heavily.
"Hello?"
"What's up?"
"Hey."
"Who was that who answered the phone?"
"That was Maureen, my new secretary."
"When did she start working there?"
"Like two weeks ago. Look we are really busy, call me later." I smacked my lips, and he held the phone in silence.
"You're not going to tell me you love me." He sighed heavily.
"I love you."
"Yeah, I love you too." While I was at the mall, I saw this nice engagement ring and I planned on going home and making things right with Mike, so I brought it and put it on my necklace just like Mike kept my ring on his.

    When I returned to Akron, I put my clothes in the house and got in my car and went down to the car wash to see who this Maureen was. When I walked in the door everyone was watching a basketball game and when I saw her, I instantly didn't like her. She had on a real tight, short sundress, not appropriate for a car wash and she was loud. Mike was sitting at his desk and Maureen was sitting on it facing the television. I walked past her and smacked my lips.
"Excuse me." Mike looked up.
"Hey, when did you get back?"

"A little while ago" and I went around on the other side of the desk next to Mike and leaned up against the desk facing him. Mike and I talked for a while and then we went outside. I saw a piece of paper lying on the desk where Maureen had been doodling her name and it read "Maureen Jenkins", so I took a mental note to ask around about her. I went home and called my girl Jeri.
"What's up girl? I need some info."
"What's up?"
"Do you know some girl named Maureen Jenkins?"
"Yeah, she went to summer school with me. Why?"
"What's up with her?"
"She's cool, but she's a hoe. She messes with this basketball player that went to school with us. She should be like eighteen. She thinks she's the shit and nobody really likes her. Why, where do you know her from?"
"She works down at Mike's car wash."
"Um…"
"What does that supposed to mean?"
"I wouldn't want her under my man because she a gold digger and if she thinks he's going to give her some money, she will fuck him."
"I'll beat that bitch's ass if she even thought about it."
"She stays over there on 22nd, her grandma or somebody gave her a house. It's green with a fence around it. It's across the street from the little street with about five houses on it.
"Good looking out. I'm going to call you later."

That Monday morning, I called the doctor and made an appointment and later found out that I was eight weeks pregnant, and the baby would be due in January. I was happy, but also sad because Mike and I weren't on the best

of terms, but I knew that was what he wanted, and I figured that was the token to get us back together. I went over his house that evening to share the news and he wasn't there, and neither was either of his cars. The guy that stayed across the street, one of his flunkies, was over there cleaning up.
"Hey you." He and I were pretty cool because Mike always had him work on my car and had me take him places for him. He came over Mike's almost every day to clean up after the dog or do something for him and I was always there.
"Hey pretty girl."
"Where's Mike?" He looked at me like I was stupid.
"He doesn't stay here anymore." I didn't show any emotion, hoping I could get more information from him.
"Oh, where does he stay now?" he started smiling.
"I'm not getting in the middle of that one." I got into my car and called Mike on his cell phone, and he answered on the first ring.
"Hello?"
"What's up?"
"Nothing…"
"Where you at?"
"At the spot. Why?"
"Because we need to talk, so where's the spot at?"
"I'll be over in a little bit." I went home and waited for two hours, and he never showed up. Now I'm pissed. I called him back.
"What?"
"Don't what me, so you supposed to have moved?"
"Yeah, but it's a business spot."
"Well, where you move to?"
"What difference do it make?"

"A whole lot of difference, I'm supposed to be your woman. Why shouldn't I know where you stay?"
"I don't have time for this" and he hung up the phone. I called him back.
"Well, I wanted to tell you that I'm pregnant."
"Yeah right..." and he hung up again and I called right back.
"You know what, fuck you Mike I'm tired of the games. The baby is due January 7th and I'll holler at you than" and I hung up.

CHAPTER- 29

I called Cleo to tell him the news because I was scared to tell my mom even though I was grown.
"Hey Cleo."
"What's up?"
"Nothing just needed to talk."
"Oh, did you enjoy your trip down here?"
"Yeah, I needed that, but I got some bad news."
"What's wrong?"
"I'm pregnant."
"By Mike?"
"Yup."
"Man, why are ya'll woman so fucking stupid?" I got quiet.
"So, when are you do?"
"January..."
"So what, are ya'll going to try to work it out?"
"I want to, but we haven't talked in a while."
"Well, if you need anything, call me."
"Thanks." It had been almost three weeks since Mike and I had spoke. I called him to inform him of my first doctor's appointment and Maureen answered his cell phone. I smacked my lips.
"Put Mike on the phone." She handed him the phone. I heard her say "Its Kya". He came to the phone.
"What's up?"
"I have a doctor's appointment tomorrow for my first check-up. Are you coming?"
"Yeah, I'll be there. Call me tomorrow and let me know where it's at and what time."
"Alright..."

I called Mike that afternoon and told him where to meet me and what time my appointment was, and he never showed up. I cried all the way home. I called him when I got home.
"Why didn't you show up?"
"What time is it?"
"It's 5:30." My appointment was at 3:30.
"I lost track of time." Then I heard Maureen in the background and the volume of the radio went up.
"I see you weren't too busy to pick her up."
"Kya, don't start."
"Look Mike, I don't want to do this by myself. You know I didn't want to have any kids before I got married."
"Hold on. Alright I'll see you tomorrow" and I heard the car door shut.
"Alright, well why don't you have an abortion?"
"You want me to kill our baby?"
"I know you're trying to go to school and all a baby is going to do is hold you down."
"I thought this was what you wanted?"
"It is, but not right now."
"What that bitch got you sprung."
"Man, she's just the secretary."
"Well, I don't want her working down there anymore."
"Okay."
"I'm not playing."
"I heard you." Mike and I ended up getting back together, even though I still didn't know where he stayed, and every time I called him Maureen was still answering his phone. I was really acting like the chicks we always talked about, the stupid chicks.
"Look Mike, I told you to get rid of her and I meant it."
"Well, you come down here and work."

"I got a real job, and you are not going to pay me what I make."
"Well, get off of it then."
"I'm not getting off it. We been through too much to let some bull shit come between us and now we got a baby on the way. Um hum. If she's not gone tomorrow, I'm out" and I hung up. Mike paged me six times and called my cell phone, but I pressed ignore and let it go to voicemail. I went over Jeri's house because he didn't know where she lived and wouldn't be able to find me. My brother Cleo was out of the Military and had come home for a couple of weeks. I came home late that night, all happy because I had had a good time playing cards with Jeri, her husband, who was my best male friend Ed, and one of his boys that went to school with us. I pulled in my driveway and got out of the car. I put my key in the door and I heard some footsteps approaching me fast. I turned around and Mike had come out of nowhere and was running in my direction. "Oh, you want to play right?" I opened the door and ran in the house. I tried to close the door, but Mike had stuck his foot in the door and was pushing it open with his body.
"Cleo!" I yelled. Cleo heard all the bumping and ran upstairs in his underwear and a 9mm in his hand. He pulled me from the door and went outside. I ran upstairs and threw my keys across the kitchen.
"Fuck!" My keys hit the wall and knocked over the sugar dish making a loud crash. My mom ran into the kitchen.
"What's wrong with you?"
"Cleo and Mike are outside and Cleo's about to shoot him." My mom ran into the living room and looked out of the window.
"It's your fault you keep running back to him." My mom didn't know I was pregnant yet. She went downstairs and

called Cleo to come in the house. I followed her but stood behind the door.

"What you gon' shoot me?" Mike asked Cleo. "Oh, you want to play dirty. I'll be back." Cleo hit him with the butt of his gun. "I'll be back nigga. I'm gon' blow this bitch up. Everybody in here is going to die tonight." Mike left and Cleo came back into the house and got his sawed-off shotgun with the red beamers on it and lied down on the floor like he was at war and waited for Mike to return. Mike continued to ride past our house throwing rocks out of the window at my car and setting off my alarm. I went to the window and pushed the button to deactivate it. When I came outside the next day I had about six dents in my car from the rocks Mike had thrown. I didn't ever call to confront him about it, because what goes around comes around and all the damage was done, and it wasn't even worth discussing.

CHAPTER- 30

I had concluded that Mike wasn't going to be there for the baby and me, so I got back into the game, but this time I was doing it big. I figured I was only three months pregnant and if I got caught, I would probably only get six months or on papers since it would be my first offence.
Jeri and I had both put in five hundred dollars a piece to get us started because she went in the game with me. One afternoon I called into work and told them that I was going to be late because I had to finish a project for school, but, in reality, I need to make a move, that was a lot more than what I made there in a week. I had a rental car because my car was in the shop getting painted and getting the dents out that Mike had put in it. I was on my way down to Edgewood when I saw Mike riding down the street with some girl in the car. I did a U turn in the Middle of Wooster, knowing I was dirty and did fifty until I caught up to him. I pulled behind him and started blowing the horn. He didn't recognize the car, so he didn't know who it was, and he kept driving. I pulled beside him and blew the horn again. He looked in my direction and I signaled for him to pull over. He stopped the car and rolled down his window and I did the same.
"Who the fuck is that bitch?"
"Ask her."
"Who are you?"
"A friend…"
"Mike ain't got no friends." I looked at Mike with a mug on my face to show him I was not playing. "Take that bitch home." Mike had done this to me one time too many and now it was my turn.

"Okay." He pulled off and I pulled off behind him. He drove back to the car wash, and she got out and started walking towards the back of the building while Mike opened his shop. I got out of my car.
"She doesn't live here." I started following her and she started running toward her car and I gave chase. She jumped in her car and pulled off. I went inside the carwash.
"Oh, nigga you want to play? You're not about to just walk out of my life while I'm carrying your baby." He picked up the phone and I snatched it out of his hand. "Oh, who you think you're calling?"
"The police…"
"Good call them, I gotta a mouth full to tell them." His cell phone rang.
"Mike is everything all right?" The girl that was in his car asked. His phone was loud, and I could hear everything that she was saying.
"Bitch, you better not call or come down here no more." I yelled in the background. She hung up the phone.
"So that's your new bitch."
"That was my new secretary, but I guess she's gone now."
"Good." I took his pager from his hip and started going through his pages. He looked at me and shook his head and picked up the phone and called my mom's phone, but Cleo answered.
"Aye man, could you come get your sister?"
"Where she at?"
"She down here tripping."
"Let me speak to her." Mike gave me the phone.
"Kya, what are you doing?"
"He had this bitch in the car."
"So, what leave that man alone and go on to where you need to be. Put Mike back on the phone." I handed him the

phone. "Do you need me to come and get her or you alright?" I was standing there with my arms folded across my chest staring at Mike.
"I think I'm alright." I went and did what I had to do, and I never made it to work.

CHAPTER- 31

Cleo left and went back to Georgia, and of course Mike and I got back together, and things were just like they were when we first met. He gave me the four hundred dollars to get my car out of the shop. He stayed the night with me at least twice a week and we went to the movies, out to dinner, or took the kids to the amusement park or something at least every weekend. Everything was good. Maureen was gone for about a month and I later found out that she had gotten pregnant by her basketball player boyfriend and when they broke up, Mike helped her get an abortion. When she returned, she was still answering his phone and always riding around in Mike's car with him, but I was naive and assumed that she knew we were together and that I was carrying his baby and Mike had told me that they weren't messing around and for some odd reason I believed him.

****

My home girl Kendra was having a surprise party for her mother and aunt who were twins. I was helping Kendra set up and get the food and stuff together and I had informed Mike of this earlier that day, because I figured we would be all afternoon. I went home to get dressed and I called Mike and we talked until I walked out of the door to go get Jeri and then go to the party. When I arrived at Kendra's mom's all her friends and family was there. We were down in the basement playing cards and shooting pool, just mingling until Kendra's aunt called and said they were on their way back. We turned out the lights and we heard them pull in the driveway. We all got in our positions and when they walked in the door we all yelled "surprise."

Her aunt had already known so she wasn't surprised, but her mom was overwhelmed. We had cake and I had a glass of wine and then Jeri and I left the party around 10:30 and we went to Roy's Place, another hood bar. I had on a sundress, and I didn't want to carry my big Coach bag in the bar, so I put my cell phone in my purse and put my purse under the back seat. Jeri and I went into the bar I order a virgin daiquiri. Jeri still didn't know that I was pregnant, and I wasn't showing yet, so I was trying to do the things that I normally did. My pager was clipped to the top of my dress, and I felt it vibrating. I looked at in and it read "111".
"Aye let me use your phone right quick." Jeri handed me her cell phone and I went outside to call Mike back.
"Why you not answering your phone?"
"I left it in the car because I don't have any pockets."
"Well come on, let's go."
"What?" I looked up and Mike was sitting across the street in his car.
"I'm not going anywhere. I'm kicking it with my girl."
"Kya, I'm not playing with you. Get your ass out here, or you're going to wish you had of."
"Whatever. Mike you always tripping. Every time I go somewhere with my girls you always, all of a sudden, want to spend time with me. You've been doing whatever all day and now you want to be bothered with me."
"I've been at work."
"Ya'll close at four o'clock and it's almost eleven."
"Whatever, just come on."
"No, I'm not going anywhere."
"Okay" and he hung up the phone. I went back inside the bar, and I must have had a worried look on my face.
"What's wrong, Kya?" asked Jeri.

"Mike out there tripping."
"Why does he act like that?"
"I don't know." I looked over at the door and Mike was trying to come in, but he had on tennis shoes, and they wouldn't let him in. He paged me again and I wasn't about to go outside where he was to call him back and the club was so noisy, we wouldn't have been able to hear each other, so I didn't call him back. The DJ stopped the music and came on the microphone.
"There's a green Sundance outside, your alarm is going off." I got up and went to the door just as my pager was going off. I still had Jeri's phone, so I called Mike back.
"So, you think I'm playing?" and he started kicking my car window. I ran across the street still holding the phone to my ear.
"Mike, what are you doing?" I got across the street and my window was shattered, the tint was the only thing that was holding it together. He snatched Jeri's phone from me and when I tried to take it back, he pushed me to the ground. I was getting up and I saw Jeri running across the street.
"Kya, get in the car let's go."
"He has your phone."
"You better give me back my phone. I don't have anything to do with what ya'll got going on."
"Bitch, I'm not giving you nothing."
"I'll show you a bitch, let me call my husband." We got into the car. "Let me see your cell phone." I got my purse from under the seat and handed her my phone. Mike came and opened my car door.
"Take her home." He saw me in my purse, and he snatched it and went and got back into his car. I wasn't even about to chase him, because I didn't feel like fighting with him. I started up my car and was headed towards Jeri's house.

"Where are you going?"
"To take you home."
"I'm not leaving you by yourself and I don't want him knowing where I live." She called her husband and told him what was going on and asked him to meet us at my house. We were going at least eighty. I was running every red light and coasting through every stop sign until I found an expressway and Mike was right on my tail.
"Where are the police when you need them?" I asked Jeri.
"You know." When I saw the expressway ramp, I accelerated to ninety. I was weaving in and out of traffic and Mike was right with me. We were afraid the window was going to fall inside of the car because it continued to shake while we were driving. When I exited the expressway, almost to my house, I told Jeri to go ahead and kick the window out and then I asked her to call my mom. She dialed the number and handed me the phone.
"Mom, Mike just kicked out my window and he took my purse and now he's chasing me in the car."
"I'm sick of this shit. Where are you?"
"On Laffer."
"Well keep riding around the blocks and I'll be there in a minute." My mom got there in a three-minute, records time. I went around two blocks, and she was there. Jeri had called Ed and told him where we were, and he said he was on his way to meet us too. I saw my mom coming down the street, so I pulled over. Mike hadn't seen her. He got out of his car and was walking towards my car when my mom stopped her truck in the middle of the street and jumped out. She still had her bed scarf on her head and her nightgown on. She had on a pair of combat boots a black trench coat and a hammer in her hand. She started walking towards Mike.

"Why don't you leave her the fuck alone? Ya'll both are getting on my damn nerves." Mike didn't say anything. He never disrespected my mom, as much as she cussed him out. "If you got her purse, give it to her."
"I don't have it" and he started walking back to his car.
"Yes, he does."
"Kya, get back in the car."
"But I need my badge to go to work Monday." Then Ed pulled up behind us and got out of his car. He had already called Jeri's phone and talked to Mike. He came over to my car and got Jeri and they both went to Mike's car, and he gave her back her phone. Jeri was no longer permitted to go anywhere with me.

When I got home my mom let me park my car in the garage so no one would steal my new CD player, my six-disk changer or my fifteen-inch speakers. A couple of weeks prior, someone had broken into Mike's Maxima and stolen his CD player and system outside of my house and I didn't want mine to get stolen too. The next day Mike called me all day, but I had turned my cell phone and my pager off, and I was screening my house calls because I didn't want to be bothered. I had taken my mom's truck and gone to the store. Mike had called while I was gone. I had changed my answer machine to a message just for him. My room door was closed and locked even though my mom didn't answer my phone or go into my room. She was down the basement when the phone rang. When the answer machine picked up, it sounded like glass was breaking and the music started playing and that's probably what caught my mom's attention.

"Can't nobody take my pride; can't nobody hold me down oh no I got to keep on moving." It was a song by Mase, and I ended it with me saying, "Leave a message."
"Oh Kya, I see you on some bull shit, so fuck you. Oh, and about the baby, hum" and he smacked his lips. I came back home and never went into my room, so I hadn't heard the message. I lied on the living room floor and fell asleep. When I woke up my mom was sitting in the living room staring at me.
"What?"
"So, you supposed to be pregnant?"
"Yup. Who told you?"
"Somebody in the street." I knew she wasn't telling the truth because nobody knew but Cleo, Mike and Kendra.
"Yeah right…" I said with a smile, and she looked at me.
"So, when are you supposed to be due?"
"In January."
"And when were you going to tell me?"
"Mike and I were going to tell you together, but then that stuff happened yesterday so…."
"So, what are you two going to do?"
"Mom I'm done and this time I'm for real." I went to work that next day and got a new badge, after I got my window fixed which was fifty-four dollars, I was planning on getting a new drivers license that evening, but Mike called me at work.
"Kya, you can come and get your purse when you get out of school."
"I'm not coming over there. I don't know where you stay anyway."
"I'm still in the same spot; I just got another spot too. You can come down to the car wash and get it."

"Nope, just keep it, you brought it anyway. I'm done and I mean it." Mike came over that evening and gave me back my purse. He continued to call me, and I continued to ignore his calls and after a while he stopped calling.

CHAPTER- 32

Jeri had a fourth of July party. I was about sixteen weeks pregnant. I had a little pouch, but I could still hide my pregnancy. I had on a sundress and a pair of high-heeled sandals that I had gotten for my birthday. I was outside helping Jeri barbeque some ribs and chicken when my cell phone rang. I looked at the caller ID and it was Kendra.
"What's up girl?"
"Where you at?"
"Across the street over Jeri's. Why what's up?"
"Mike just came over here and said that you must have had some nigga over here and that's why you were hiding your car." Just as she was talking my pager went off and it was Mike.
"He just paged me, but I'm not calling him back. What did you tell him?"
"I told him that you weren't over here, but he didn't believe me."
"Oh well. Thanks for letting me know what's up. I'll talk to you later."
As soon as we got the food almost together it started drizzling so we moved the party inside her apartment. I got ready to leave around 11:30 that night and when I got outside, I had two flat tires.
"Son of a bitch!" I went back into the house and called Triple A but I only had one spare so they could only change one tire. They came out, and my spare was buried under my speakers and when I moved everything out of the way my tire was rusted, and it took him almost a half an hour get it out. I called my mom.
"Mom, I need you to come and get me."

"Where are you?"
"Over Jeri's."
"Down in Edgewood?"
"Yup."
"What are you doing down there this late? And what's wrong with your car?"
"I mysteriously got two flats. I know Mike did it because he went over Kendra's house looking for me. I called Triple A, and they came out and changed one of my tires, but I didn't have another spare."
"I'll be over there in a minute." I went back into the house and while I waited for my mom, I called Mike.
"You are a sorry ass nigga. How the fuck are you going to slash my tires and leave me stranded when you know I'm pregnant?"
"What are you talking about?"
"Don't play dumb, somebody told me they saw your car over here."
"Do you need me to come and get you?"
"Nope, but I see how you are though. You don't give a fuck about me or mine" and I hung up. When my mom got there, she couldn't get the tire off and Ed and his boys had left, they said they were going riding. They were tired of Mike bothering me for no reason and they were going to take care of him. My mom called my granddad, and he came over there, and she gave me her spare tire so that I could get my car home. I didn't talk to Mike again until I was seven months pregnant. I did everything in my power to stay away from him.

CHAPTER- 33

I was now seven and a half months pregnant, and my stomach had really started to poke out and my coworkers started to notice and a few weeks later my company said, *"they were downsizing"* and they let me go. I went downtown and applied for unemployment, but I was denied because they said that it was a high school assignment, even though I had graduated three and a half years ago. I saw a sign that the US Postal Service was hiring for Christmas help. I filled out an application and was hired two weeks later. I got myself together and left the street life in the streets. I had almost ten thousand dollars saved up. I brought two CD's and put three thousand dollars in each one, at a three percent interest rate and I put the rest in my savings account. I figured if I worked for the next month and a half, I would have enough money to get my baby anything she wanted and needed if her dad didn't want to be a part of our lives. When I applied for the job, I didn't tell them that I was pregnant, but during my orientation one of the group leaders noticed and made me go and tell the head and they put me on light duty. I worked from 5pm until 3 or 4 in the morning. I had withdrawn from my class at the University because I was having a few problems with the baby and I was taking some very challenging courses and I had missed a lot of classes, so I usually came home and slept until it was time for me to get ready to go back to work. I had met a guy at work who I had been checking out in my orientation class named Nick. I thought he was nice looking but I wasn't trying to start up anything when I knew I was about to have another man's baby.

One evening I was sitting in the break room eating a pack of saltine crackers and drinking a cup of ice water when Nick walked in. He came over to the table and sat down beside me.
"What up Kya? I know that's not your lunch."
"Naw, I ate earlier."
"Dang, you're sitting there looking extra sexy."
"Man, I'm all fat."
"But you look good. I would love to hold them titties them big two knobs and start nuttin' in your ass in big goo gobs." I cut my eyes at him and got up and threw the ice water I was drinking in his face along with the cup, then I went back to my workstation. From that day forward we were very good friends. He started telling everybody that he was my baby daddy, so wouldn't anyone try to talk to me.

Mike called me one afternoon while I was getting ready for work.
"Hey Kya, how you been?"
"Fine." I answered dryly.
"How's the baby?"
"She's alright."
"So, we're having a girl."
"Yup."
"She's going to be so pretty, just like her mom."
"Um, what's up?"
"Can you do me a favor?"
"What?"
"I need a ride down to Century, so that I can get my truck." I looked at the clock and I still had an hour before it was time for me to go to work and I hadn't seen him in a while, and just hearing his voice made me kind of miss him and I knew he would do it for me.

"You ready now?"
"Yeah, met me down at the store." I went down to his store, and he was standing in the doorway waiting. He got into the car, and we drove down to Century's. When I pulled in the parking lot, I left the car running.
"You're not going to wait with me?"
"No, I have to go to work." He gave me a distraught look.
"Where do you work?"
"The Post Office."
"For real?"
"Yup." He gave me a disappointed look. He reached over and rubbed my stomach, while he kissed me on the cheek. For the past three months, I hadn't thought much about Mike. You know what they say out of sight out of mind, but when I saw him, he was looking so fine, and all those old feelings came rushing back. He looked like he had just had a fresh haircut. He had on a pair of tan khakis and a Nike sweater that I had brought him last Christmas.
"Alright, well I'm going to call you later, okay?"
"Alright..." I was trying to act all nonchalant. He got out of the car, and I pulled off. He stood in the parking lot and watched me until I couldn't see him anymore.

      I was leaving work, when my pager went off. I looked at it, wondering who could be calling me at 2:30 in the morning, and it was Mike. I called him back.
"Why are you up so late?"
"I was chillin' with my dudes."
"Why don't you come down to the spot and chill for a little while, or are you tired?"
"No, I'm wide awake. I usually don't go to bed until about fourish."

"Well come through." He gave me the address to his spot. I got there and I thought I had the wrong house because the driveway had about four cars in it and there were cars lined up the street like someone was having a party. I called him back to verify the address and I had the right house. He let me in but prohibited me to go down the basement where he was running an after hour.

"Aye man" I heard him call to one of his boys. "Can you handle this for me?" He and I went upstairs to his bedroom and reminisced the past in more ways than one and we fell asleep in each other's arms. The next morning, we went to Big Boy's and ate breakfast.

"Kya, I want us to be a family. Can we try to work this out?"

"Do you feel like you're ready for that?"

"I know I am."

"Alright, time will tell." Inside I was jumping with joy, but I would never let him know how ecstatic I was. I went home and took a nap before it was time for me to get ready for work. I sat at my workstation and thought about if this was what I really wanted to do. I had a couple of friends that I talked to, but no one I had to answer to and I was comfortable with that, but I wanted a family and decided to give Mike another chance.

CHAPTER- 34

I woke up at 3 am because my body felt weird. I wasn't in a lot of pain; I just didn't feel right. I went into the bathroom and took a warm bath to relax my muscles.
"Kya?" My mom called from her bedroom.
"Yeah?"
"What are you doing?"
"Just taking a bath."
"Are you alright?"
"Yeah, my back was hurting a little bit and the baby won't be still."
"Girl, you probably in labor, get out that tub, that warm water can make the baby come out and you'll have it right there in that tub." I washed my body real fast and got out. When I came out of the bathroom my mom was up. She was sitting on her bed with the light on.
"So, do you want me to call off of work?"
"For what?"
"In case you have the baby today."
"I'm not due until tomorrow."
"Well she might come early."
"Naw, I don't want you to waste a day. Go ahead and go to work. I'll call Mike."
"Are you sure?"
"Yeah." I paged Mike and he got there at 6:30 am. He made me breakfast in bed, which was a juicy steak and eggs. Then he made love to me very slowly so he wouldn't hurt the baby or me. We lied down and watched cartoons until it was time to pick his daughter up from school at 3:15. I kept feeling little pains, but the doctor told me to stay at home until I had a pain that made me cry. I told him I had a high tolerance for pain, but I guess he didn't believe

me. Mike was getting on his coat when I had another sharp pain in my stomach.
"Ouch." I grabbed my stomach. "Mike, I think I better go to the hospital."
"Alright come on. I have to go pick up Divine from school first." I called my mom while I got on my coat and shoes. We picked up Divine and headed to the hospital.

   When we arrived, I walked in and went to the counter to check in.
"Yes, may I help you?"
"Yes, I'm in labor."
"Excuse me?"
"I'm in labor." She looked down at my stomach.
"Are you sure?" Mike started laughing.
"Yeah, she is."
"Okay let me get you a wheelchair."
"That's Okay, I can walk."
"I'm sorry that's our procedure." They wheeled me up to a room and Mike and Divine followed.
"Ma'am, I need you to try to use the restroom and take off your clothes and put on this gown." I did what I was told and came out of the bathroom and sat down on the table.
"Lie down and scoot all the way to the end of the table and put your feet in the stirrups." I gave Mike a crazy look.
"Oh, let me take Divine home and I'll be right back." He and Divine left. I lie down on the table and put my feet in the stirrups. The lady stuck her hand inside of me and pressed down on my stomach.
"Oh my gosh."
"What's wrong?"
"The baby is coming now. Why did you wait so long before you came to the hospital?"

"Well, my doctor told me to stay at home until I had a pain that brought a tear to my eyes."
"Stupid." She shook her head. She hurriedly put IVs in my arm. She kept messing up; she had blood running all down my arm and on the floor. "I'm so sorry; I'm trying to hurry up." She finally got it right and wheeled me down to the delivery room. By the time they got the rest of my IV's in and called the doctor, who was out of town, my mom and Mike were there. We were sitting in the delivery room waiting for my doctor's substitute to get there when I felt another sharp pain.
"Mom, I'm supposed to get an epidural."
"It's not time yet."
"My contractions are two minutes apart. When am I supposed to get it?"
"Just wait." I was lying there talking to Mike when I had a real hard contraction.
"Ouch!" I yelled and I started crying. My water had broken and then I threw up the steak and eggs I had eaten for breakfast. My mom left the room to get the nurse.
"Are you alright?"
"No. I was supposed to get an epidural, and no one's given it to me." She looked at my chart.
"You're right, I see it right here, but your contractions are too close. I don't think it will kick in on time."
"I don't care just give it to me anyway." She got the supplies and handed me a pillow and had me sit on the edge of the bed and arch my back while holding the pillow. She took this long needle out of this paper filled with a liquid that looked like water.
"Don't look because you might panic."
"I'm not afraid of needles." She got beside me and stuck that six-inch needle into my spine.

"Don't move." It pinched, put it didn't hurt that badly.
"I gave you a little extra dosage. Hopefully it will kick in, in time." I lied back on the bed and watched my contractions on the monitor. I still felt them, but they didn't hurt as badly and twenty minutes later I gave birth to a beautiful six-pound, eight-ounce little girl. When the baby came out Mike had a mean mug on his face because the baby was lighter complected. She kind of looked Chinese and Mike is darker than I am.
"Aren't you going to call your mom?" My mom asked.
"Oh yeah" he called his mom and told her he had another girl. He named her Mikyah Mack, after him and me.

The next three days seemed like the longest days of my life, but Mike made my stay nice. He came to the hospital and stayed two of the nights with the baby and me, and he showered us with gifts. Just looking at him hold and love his daughter made me think he was the best father on this earth, and I loved him more than I ever did.

When they said I could leave the hospital, I almost ran out of the door.
"Ma'am." One of the nursed called. "We have to wheel you and the baby out."
"I've been walking around here for the past three days, I'm sure I can make it out of here."
"I know, but its procedure." I sat down in the chair and Mike and my mom wheeled me outside. I rode home with my mom since we were going to the same place. I went into my room and my mom had everything set up beautifully. She wouldn't let me do anything, so I went into the bathroom and took a sitz bath to clean my stitches, that my big head baby caused me to get because she split me. I

went into my room and lied down and watched TV. I must have dozed off and was awaken by the ringing phone. I thought it was Mike, so I answered it.
"Hey Kya, what's up?"
"Nothing. Who is this?"
"Dang, you don't know my voice?"
"Look I don't feel like playing."
"It's me, Nick. I heard you had our little girl."
"Yeah, I had her. Who told you?"
"I got my resources."
"Oh."
"So can I come and see her?"
"No, I'm in the bed and I don't feel like getting up. I just got home a couple of hours ago."
"So, are you saying I can't see my daughter."
"What are you on? Look I'm about to go back to sleep, so holla back" and I hung up. I was eight months pregnant when I met Nick and we had never slept together. He had some issues, more than I could handle.

    For the next month Mike was there to see his baby everyday. He brought one of his boys over to see her and he never let his friends know where I lived. Between Mike and me, Mikyah had every pair of Nikes and Jordan's that was out for kids, and she was always dressed to impress. I had gone down to the University and registered for classes because I'm the type to finish what I started, and one member of my family had called my mom one day and I answered her phone.
"Kya, is your mom home?"
"No, she's not, but how are you doing?"
"I'm fine. Now girl, you know you done messed up your life having that baby and don't ask me to baby-sit because I

don't. You're not going to get a chance to finish school and you're going to be on the welfare for the rest of your life." That really hurt me, but I was never one to let another individual steal my dreams. That negatively only made me want to strive harder. My classes were usually over around at 11:30 am and I didn't work so I spent a lot of time with Trina and my niece who had recently moved to Ohio or kicking it with my girls. Everything was going well, and it was my spring break and Mike and I wanted to get away. We got on the Greyhound and headed to Canada. We were hugging, kissing and rubbing each other all the way there like we were teenagers. We got to the boarder between New York and Canada and the bus stopped.

"Everyone will need to get your luggage and please exit the bus through the front door." There were a lot of moans and groans, but everyone got off the bus. We had to stand in a line, and they checked everyone, one by one to see if anyone had a warrant or a felony. Mike had several felonies. They sent us to a different room with one other guy in it and everyone else got back on the bus and we saw the bus pull off.

"Could you two come with me?" a medium built gray-headed guy asked. We followed him into a small room. He looked at Mike.

"Do you mind if she stays in here? Mike shrugged his shoulders. "Well Mr. Mack, you know I can take you to jail, and you'll be there for the weekend."

"For what?"

"You're a felon and you're not allowed to cross the border."

"Well, I didn't know. I was just trying to spend some time with my girl."

"Do you want to explain these felonies?"

"Most of them are from a long time ago, but I've grown up." I got up and went back in the other room and a lady was going through our luggage.
"Ma'am, do either of you have any weapons, illegal drugs, or alcohol in your luggage?"
"No." She continued to check our luggage then she called a cab that took us to the bridge and let us out. We walked about eight miles before we found a decent hotel. We passed about six motels that were full of mouse holes in the wall, or the doorknobs were hanging off and I refused to stay there. We made the best out of our trip and ended up having a lovely time. Mike and I were lying in the bed with the champagne I had brought with us.
"Mike, I really want to make this work. You said you wanted us to be a family and so do I." I pulled out the ring I had brought from Georgia. "So, what's up?" Mike took the ring.
"Oh baby, this is nice."
"So can I have my ring back?"
"What ring?"
"The one on your necklace."
"No, I can't do that right now."
"Why not?"
"I just can't."
"Well give me my ring back."
"No, you gave it to me."
"Well by accepting that ring means you're accepting a commitment." He didn't say anything he just put the ring on his finger.

New York's time was an hour different than ours, and we didn't know. I overheard a man say it was 3:30. I looked at my watch and it read 2:30.

"Excuse me sir, did you say it was 3:30?"
"Yes, New York's time is an hour different." We ran back to the hotel and grabbed our luggage and took a cab to the bus station, but we had missed the bus. We had to wait two hours to be put on the next bus. This was one of the worst trips I had ever had in my life, and I couldn't wait to get home.

A week after we returned word had gotten to me that Maureen was supposed to be pregnant by Mike. I didn't ask him because I knew he would lie, and he once told me that he would lie to me to spear my feelings. I started hanging around at the car wash everyday where she was working again. Mike still treated me like I was his woman even in front of her, so I didn't believe it. After about a month or two Maureen stopped coming to work and I continue to hear the rumors, so I went to Mike.

"So is Maureen supposed to be pregnant by you and don't lie?"

"Man, no and stop coming at me with this bull shit." I could tell when Mike was lying so I decided to pay Maureen a little visit. Jeri didn't give me Maureen's address, but she described the house to me very well. I rode up and down her street until I found a house that matched the description Jeri had given me and it looked vacant. There were a few guys standing outside in front of the house on the wall.

"Excuse me, does Maureen live here?" They all shook their heads no and one of them said she moved.

"Do you know where she moved to?" They all looked at each other.

"With her baby's dad, Mike." My heart melted. I knew Mike had moved but she didn't stay there because I was over there all the time. I called Mike at the car wash.
"He's not here." One of his workers said. "Who is this?"
"This is Kya."
"The girl with the green car?"
"Yeah."
"Oh, he went bowling."
"Alright." I hung up and called Mike's cell phone, but he didn't answer so I paged him '911'. I paged Mike about thirty times between 2 pm and 9 pm and he didn't call me back. I was so frustrated I flipped. I went down to his house and banged on the door, but he wasn't there. I went down to this carwash, where he had also started selling used cars, and put sugar in four of the gas tanks to make sure he wouldn't make any money from them. He was going to pay a high price to play me again. I went over his sister's house because he was good for hiding over there. I saw his truck, but I didn't see his car. I parked my car three driveways away from where his truck was parked. I got my razor out of my glove compartment and ran down to his truck and stabbed his tire and my blade broke. I retracted it a little bit and slashed his tire so that it couldn't be repaired. I was going to slash two of them like he did me, but the first one made so much noise it made the neighborhood dogs bark, and I had my baby in the car, I couldn't take a chance in getting caught. I got back home and paged Mike with '111-111-5537-2' which meant two less people he had to worry about in his life. I lied down and cried myself to sleep. Once again Mike had hurt me.

CHAPTER- 35

My first Mother's Day Mike had promised me he would spend the day with me. I called him that morning and he didn't answer his phone, so I paged him. I started getting dressed for the day while I waited for him to return my call. He ended up calling me at 3:30 and by this time I had other plans to go the Cedar Point with Antwon and his boys.
"I thought you were going to spend the day with me, it's my first Mother's Day?"
"I was asleep."
"Oh, well can you watch your daughter so I can go do something?"
"Nope, I'm spending the day with my mom."
"Well, she can chill with ya'll."
"I said no." and he hung up the phone. I packed Mikyah's diaper bag, put her on a sweater and put her in her car seat and we drove to Mike's mom's house. I got out and knocked on the door. His mom let me in and wouldn't you know Maureen was sitting in the dining room. Mike came out of the kitchen and stopped in his tracks when he saw me standing there. I wasn't the one to put on a show in front of another female, but I had a few choice words for Mike.
"Come outside for a minute." He followed me out the door.
"So that's why you couldn't spend the day with me or keep your daughter because you up in that bitch's face? You are going to keep your daughter because I got something to do." I took Mikyah out of the car and Mike jumped into his car and locked the doors.
"You a sorry nigga, I see you want to play games." He started up his car and started backing out of the driveway,

leaving me standing there with the baby. I put the baby back in the car and tried to follow him, but he got on the highway, and I lost him. I went back home to mope, like I had been doing lately. When I got in the house the light on my answering machine was blinking. I was going to just press delete and not even listen to it because I thought it was Mike, but I decided against it. I pressed play.
"Aye Kya, I hope this is your number, this is Jonel. Your girl gave me your number. If this is you and you get a chance call me." He left his cell number and his pager number. Jonel was a guy that I used to like a lot when I was in school, but he went to East with me, so that made him off limits. I called him right back.
"Hey Jonel, this is Kya."
"Oh, what's up girl?"
"Nothing same ole' shit just a different day."
"I heard that."
"So, which one of my friends gave you, my number?"
"Leona. I had to give her a twenty sack to get it." That made my day.
"Oh, she sold me out for a twenty sack. I gotta to talk to her." We both laughed.
"So can I see you today?"
"Let me see if I can find a babysitter for an hour or two. I'll call you back." I called Trina.
"What are you doing?"
"Nothing, just watching TV."
"Where is Taytay?"
"In her room."
"Can you keep Mikyah for a couple of hours?"
"Where are you going?"
"On a date."
"With Mike?"

"Naw, he's with his new bitch. I found something else to get into, or should I say something else found me."
"About time. Yeah, I'll watch that little dwarf." I dropped Mikyah off and met Jonel at the park. We talked and reminisced the past for the whole two hours. I hadn't laughed or smiled that much in months. Jonel and I became very good friends. I would go to his job on his breaks, and we would sit back and talk. He would come over and make sure that Mikyah or I didn't need anything and after a while I realized I didn't need Mike. I started looking for an apartment and I found a nice two bedroom right around the corner from my mom that was perfect. My brothers and their boys moved me in a two-hour record time, and they even went to the furniture store to pick up my dinette set that I had brought. I had my phone transferred to my apartment and I didn't tell Mike that I had moved.

A couple of weeks had gone by, and I guess it had finally hit Mike that I wasn't fucking with him anymore. He called me one morning about 7:30.
"Where are you at?"
"At home."
"Where is your car?"
"In the driveway."
"Well, I'm outside, come open the door."
"You're outside of where my mom's house? Oh, I don't live there anymore."
"Where do you live at?"
"It doesn't matter, if you want to see us, we'll meet you down at the car wash or we'll come over your house."
"Don't come down to my job and don't come over my house."

"Alright, you said it."
"You are a stupid bitch."
"I know and a good one too" he hung up on me. I rolled over feeling like a new woman.

      I had gotten bored sitting at home all day, so I decided to find a job. I needed Mike to baby-sit because the daycare closed at 6:30 and I didn't get off until 9. I went to school in the morning and work in the evening, so my days were busy, and I didn't have time to think about Mike's bullshit. I went to pick Mikyah up one evening and no one was at Mike's house. I called him from my cell phone, but he didn't answer so I paged him and went home. He called me back about fifteen minutes later, enough time for me to get home.
"Where ya'll at?"
"I had to go somewhere. I'll bring her home. Where do you stay?"
"I'll come get her just go to the house."
"I'm going to bring her home or you won't see her." I said forget it. I gave him the address and he brought her home.

      Mike pulled his car all the way to the back and came in the house and sat down on the couch.
"It looks like you been staying here a minute."
"Yeah, something like that."
"Can I use the bathroom?"
"Yeah, it's the first door at the top of the stairs." He went upstairs and was gone for a good five minutes. I went upstairs to check on him and he had taken off his clothes and gotten into my bed.
"What are you doing?"
"Come lay down with me."

"Uh um you got to go."
"I'm not going anywhere." I went downstairs and got my baby and brought her upstairs. I was lying across the bed talking to Mike when I heard someone knock at the door.
"Who knows where you live?"
"I don't know." I knew it had to have been Jonel because he was the only one that knew where I stayed.
Mike opened the picture window in my bedroom.
"Yeah?" Jonel looked up.
"Is Tracy here?"
"You got the wrong house." Mike closed the window and looked at me. I shrugged my shoulders and turned my head. I wanted to tell him that I had moved on, but Mike had this serious mind control thing over me. I think I was afraid of him. He lied back down and started kissing me in the mouth. I didn't resist and I kissed him back. He stuck his hand down my pants and penetrated me. He pulled up my shirt and unhooked my bra and slowly sucked on my nipples. He licked me all the way down to my belly button while he slowly pulled down my pants. He kissed my inner thighs then wrapped his arms around my legs and went into that creamy center of love. He licked and sucked me so good that tears started rolling down my face. I really missed this good loving. After I climaxed, he stuck his manhood inside of me and looked me in the eyes.
"So, you had another nigga around you and my baby?" Then he came down with a hard stroke. "Huh?" I started moaning. "You my baby and I don't want nobody in your face" and he hit it hard again. We had sex for a good hour because the love was gone for me, I just didn't want to fight or argue with him, so I just went with the flow. From that day forward Mike was at my house almost every night. He paid for me to get my phone number changed and I

disconnected my cell phone and I never seen or heard from Jonel again. Another good man lost.

CHAPTER- 36

During the time Mike was staying with me, Maureen had her baby. He had moved her out to Cuyahoga Falls away from everybody and no one knew she had a baby. He took her away from her family and she didn't have a phone or a car, so she was stuck in the house until Mike decided to check on her. I had gone down to the car wash one Saturday morning and it was the first time I'd been down there in a while because school and work kept me busy. On the back wall of Mike's car wash was "his wall of fame" and he had pictures of all ten of his kids hanging on the wall. There was a picture of a newborn baby hanging up there too. I walked over and looked at the picture.
"Who is this?"
"That's my sister's baby."
"I just saw your sister, and she didn't just have a baby." I took the picture from the wall. "So that bitch did have a baby by you" and I ripped it up and threw it in the trash. Mike ran over to me and pushed me down on the couch. He went outside and got into his car and left me at his shop.

A couple weeks prior I had gotten an application in the mail from the US Postal Services wanting me to reapply. I had filled it out and sent it back and when I came home that evening, I had my welcoming package in the mail, and I was to start in two weeks.

Mikyah and I were outside, I was sitting on my stoop and Mikyah was riding in her Barbie power wheel jeep, when I saw Mike's truck pulling in the driveway. Mikyah had gotten so big; she was a little over nine months

and had started walking not to long ago. She saw her daddy and got out of her jeep and ran towards his truck. "Daddy!" He got out and picked her up and kissed her. I couldn't take it because they were so happy around each other. I got up and went into the house and sat on the steps. Mike came in the house carrying the baby and he looked at me and I rolled my eyes. Mike knew I wouldn't trip on him in front of my daughter because she was smart, and I would never turn her against him. She'd see who he really was as she grew up. He put her down and she ran and got on her scoot n' go and started pushing the buttons. Mike stood in front of the steps.
"What do you want?" I asked in a low tone.
"Kya, I know that I hurt you, again. I'm just a fuck up and I'm sorry for being the person that I am."
"You damn right you're sorry. You're sorry and you're weak" and I rolled my eyes at him.
"Kya, I want us to get married and have another baby."
"You just had a baby. Ooh and then you are going to tell me to have an abortion and then you go get that bitch pregnant?"
"I told you I wanted you to finish school."
"And I told you that a baby doesn't stop no show, at least not this one. That bitch is sorry just like you and she's not going to amount to shit. Ya'll deserve each other. I'm done, you have hurt me one time to many, and I just keep forgiving your ass." By this time tears were running down my face.
"Baby we can work this out. Things will be different I promise. You are my world. You mean everything to me."
"Things are not going to get better because I'm not about to have that little bastard sitting up in my face or my daughter's. As far as I am concerned, he doesn't exist."

"That's my responsibility not yours and you don't have to ever worry about him being around you" and he started crying along with me.
"Mike I'm sorry but I'm through. My heart can't take anymore. You're more than welcome to see your daughter anytime you want, just call before you come by."
"Kya, you can't leave me. I love you and I need you."
"You got her now, so you do you."
"I don't want to be with her, if I did, I wouldn't be over her kissing your ass."
"Well, you showed me that you didn't want me so, I'm out of your way." We continued our conversation and Mike finally left after an hour of getting nowhere.

****

  My girl and I had gone shopping and I ended up being an hour late for work. When I walked in the door the supervisor tried to front.
"Don't even clock in, you're an hour late. Look how busy we are. You can turn around and go back to where you came from." I wasn't mad. My mom had started watching Mikyah, so I went over there and picked her up. When I got my check that Friday, I told them I wasn't coming back.

  My first day at my new job was great. Everybody had remembered me from when I had worked there when I was pregnant, so I got the good jobs and I fit right in. They ended up keeping me until June, which was another six months, and I made some good money and was able to get unemployment when my assignment was over. I only saw my daughter two or three hours a day and on Thursday's when I didn't go to school or work. My classes started at 7:45 am and were over at 11 am. Mikyah was in daycare during that time, but sometimes I would leave her there longer so that I could do my homework and take a nap. I worked from 5 pm until 1:30 am depending on the workload and by the time I picked up my baby and went home it was close to 2 am. That semester I graduated with a 3.8 GPA with a degree in Computer Programming. I was so proud of myself, and I proved everyone wrong that had doubts about me pursuing my career. Mike had called me a few days before my ceremony and asked could he attend. I had an extra ticket, and I didn't mind because we were still cool, but we just weren't a couple, but he took good care of his daughter and I, so I gave him a ticket. She didn't want for anything and neither did I. After the ceremony Mike took me to my favorite restaurant, we ate dinner and had a couple of drinks then went back to my house where he stayed the night. We were in bed and my phone rang. I got up and ran downstairs to answer it and they hung up. I figured they must have had the wrong number. This went on for the next two weeks so finally I pressed *69 and I wrote down the number. I hung up the phone and dialed the number back. The phone rang five times and then the answering machine picked up.

"Hi, this is Maureen and Mikel sorry we missed your call. Leave a message..." and I hung up. Mike and I had decided to give this love thing another try, and I thought that since he was now thirty maybe he'd grown up and he'd change for me.

CHAPTER- 37

After my graduation Mike had half-way moved in with me, but he didn't have all his things there just a few of them, but he slept there every night. I had gotten a day job in the office of a bank, so I was home every evening. Maureen had started playing on my phone on the regular and I wasn't about to pay fifty dollars to get my number changed for her to get it again, so I got privacy management, where if you called from a private number, you had to say your name before your call would go through. Then she started playing games saying that she was calling from Planned Parenthood. I knew I had never been there, so I played her game.

"Hi Kya, this is Sue calling from Planned Parenthood."
"Hi Sue. What can I do for you?"
"I need you to come down to our office."
"Oh really, what's the problem?"
"We would like to tell you in person."
"Okay. So, Sue, tell me how did you get my number, considering I have never been to Planned Parenthood? Now bitch stop calling my house" and I hung up. The next day I got a call from the Health Clinic, and it was a man asking me to call. I returned his call.
"Ma'am we need you to come down to the clinic and get tested for syphilis."
"Why, what's the problem? I never been down there before and how did you get my number?"
"Someone you came in contact with gave us your number."
"Who?"
"I can't revel that information, but I need you to come to get tested." Just to be on the safe side, I made an appointment, and my results were negative. I don't know if

that was one of Maureen's games or not because the only person, I had been with was Mike and when I questioned him about it, he acted like he didn't know what I was talking about and accused me of being with someone else. The silly games people play for attention.

****

I woke up one morning around 6:00 and Mike wasn't there, and he hadn't called me all night. I called his cell phone and got his voicemail, and then I paged him. I put on a pair of jeans and Mikyah, and I went to his house but he wasn't there so he couldn't lie and say he was asleep. I got back to the house and was about to page him again when he walked in the door.
"Where you been all night?"
"Working," his breath reeked of liquor. "Come lay down with me."
"I have to get ready for work."
"I'll pay you for the day, now lay down" and he pushed me on the bed. I laid there for a minute because I knew he would be asleep real soon. When I heard him snoring, I got up and went through his pager because I knew he was with somebody else. I felt it in my heart. The last page before my three was from a number I recognized, but couldn't remember where I knew it from, followed by 69-69. I got up and went downstairs to call the number back. I dialed the number, and the phone rang five times and then an answering machine picked up.
"Hi this is Maureen and..." and I hung up. I went back upstairs and pulled the covers off Mike.
"Get the fuck up and get out."
"Man gone."

"I'm not playing. I told you if you ever cheated on me again it was over."
"Ain't nobody cheating on you."
"Then why the fuck is Maureen paging you with a sixty-nine? She wanted you to come over so she can suck your dick and you went running." I started walking out of my room. "Be gone when I get back or I'm calling the police." He got up and ran after me and grabbed me by the collar of my shirt and had my back against the wall. I started pushing him and I kneed him in the stomach, and he smacked me in the mouth, when I tasted the blood in my mouth, I had flash backs of the fight we had and started thinking about how much I loved him, how he keeps hurting me and I keep being quiet about it. He pulled me back into my bedroom by my arm and pushed me onto the bed and started trying to unbuckle my pants.
"Get off of me" and I started kicking him and then the baby started crying. "Let me go see about the baby."
"She alright." I continued to try to fight him off. "You fucking somebody else that's why you don't want to give me none?"
"No, you are that's why I'm not fucking you." He had me lying on the bed on my back. He was sitting on my thighs with one of his hands around my neck chocking me while he was unbuckling my pants with the other. I was trying to pull his hands from my neck because I couldn't breathe, but that only made him choke me harder. I was determined not to give him any sex, but after a while I gave up the fight. My vagina wasn't wet because I didn't want it, but after he penetrated me, it got moist.
"Oh, baby you got some good pussy. Uh I love my pussy." I just laid there and finally he came inside of me. He rolled off top of me and fell asleep. I lay there another few

minutes and went to check on Mikyah, who she was sitting on her toddler bed playing with her toys. I had taken her crib down because she kept jumping out of it. I went into the bathroom searching for something; I just didn't know what it was.
I found a bottle of rubbing alcohol and went downstairs, taking Mikyah with me. I sat her on the bottom step. "Mommy will be right back" and I kissed her on the forehead. I grabbed my lighter off the top of the entertainment center, I used for my incense, and I walked calmly back upstairs. I opened the bottle of alcohol and looked around the room. I went over to the bed and knocked all the candles over on the bed, so it would look like an accident. I poured the alcohol all over the cover that Mike was lying under.
"This mutha fucka think he can just go out and cheat on me and then come in here and smack me around, and then make me fuck him. This is the last straw. I'm tired." Then I set the bed on fire. I went downstairs and called Shawn. "Girl, I don't know what just came over me, but I just set the bed on fire, with Mike in it."
"Whatever."
"I'm not playing. What should I do?"
"Why are you going to burn down your shit? You better put that shit out before your ass go to jail and then you are going to have more things to worry about and he still will be doing his dirt."
I'll call you back." I went back upstairs, and the flames were just beginning to blaze up and Mike was still asleep. I went into the bathroom and grabbed some towels and some water, and I tried to smoother the flames. When I turned around Mikyah was standing there with her mouth open.

"Leave my daddy alone" and she started crying and Mike woke up.
"What the fuck?" he yelled while jumping out of the bed. I grabbed Mikyah and ran downstairs and out the door. I went to the grocery store and brought some milk and just walked around the store to clear my head. When I got ready to go back home, I couldn't find my keys. I went outside and looked in my car window, but they weren't in there. I went back into the store and went to the customer service desk and called Mike, but he didn't answer the house phone and his cell phone was off because when I called it, it went straight to voicemail. I called the house phone again and my answering machine picked up.
"Mike this is me, would you please pick up the phone?" I waited a few seconds and hung up and called right back.
"Hello?" he answered.
"Mike, I need you to do me a favor."
"What baby?"
"I can't find my keys. Can you come and get me?"
"Where are you?"
"At the grocery store" then a lady came on the loudspeaker.
"I have a set of keys at the customer service desk." I looked up at her.
"Hey, do they have a green long key chain on them?"
"Yes."
"Those are mine."
"Never mind Mike, they found them." It seemed like every time I tried to leave Mike something would go wrong, and I would need him for something. I went back home to take my milk home and see if Mike had left. I went upstairs to my bedroom to see the damages and Mike was sitting on the edge of the bed. All the covers had burn holes all over them and Mike's boxer shorts were all burned up. When I

walked in the room, he looked at me, but he didn't say anything. I was afraid he was going to call the police because he had a deranged look on his face. I picked up his pants from the floor and took his keys out of his pockets so that he couldn't go anywhere, and he never moved. He just kept watching me out of the corner of his eye. I grabbed Mikyah's diaper bag and went outside and got into Mike's truck and took her to daycare and I went to work. I finally had the control, and he didn't know how to take it.

    I had already called my supervisor and told her that I would be late. When I arrived, my eyes were still red and puffy from my crying and my lip was swollen. I went to my supervisor's desk to sign in.
"Kya are you alright?" I shook my head yes and I started crying. She got up and hugged me.
"Are you alright to work?" I shook my head yes. She looked down at my clothes. "I hate to be the barrier of bad news, but today is not a jean day." I had forgotten to change my clothes.
"I'm sorry. I just had a rough morning. I'll go home on my break and change. I don't live that far from here." I lived about twenty minutes away, but I didn't clock in or out, so I left when I wanted to all the time anyways.

    When it was time for me to take my break, I went outside and got into Mike's Jeep. I was driving down the street heading towards my house when the car shut off. I started it back up and the gaslight was on, but I hadn't noticed. The gas station was about five minutes away in the car. I tried to hurry, but I was caught in traffic and as soon as I turned onto Exchange Street, the car shut off again and this time I couldn't get it back started. I walked to a shop downtown and tried to call Mike and again he didn't answer the phone. I paged him, called his cell phone and my house phone and nothing. I walked back down to the truck hoping I'd maybe see someone that I knew. Several police cars rode past and just looked. I got frustrated and walked back downtown and called the police station. After an hours wait, an officer came and gave me a ride to the gas station. He made me sit in the back like I was a criminal. I saw him run Mike's license plate and a list of items came up.

"Oh, that's not my car?" He didn't say anything. I knew a lot of the police officers from attending the policeman's ball and from bowling, so I started a conversation.

"So how is Sergeant Straiten doing?"

"Which one?"

"Paul."

"Oh, he's good." We made it to the gas station, and he paid for my gas and a gas can, took me back down to the truck, put the gas in the truck for me and gave me the can. He followed me back to the gas station so that I could put some more gas in the truck. It was funny how when he thought I was just some thug on the street he treated me that way, but when he found out I knew his sergeant, his whole demeanor changed.

When I finally made it home Mike wasn't there. I changed my clothes and went back to work. Mike came and picked up his truck that evening and for the next few months, he was on his best behavior, and we started looking for us a house to raise our family in.

CHAPTER- 38

After looking at what seemed like one hundred houses Mike, and I finally agreed upon a nice three-bedroom house with a very large yard. It needed some minor repairs, but nothing that we couldn't handle together. Mike was supposed to have had everything moved before I came home from work, but when I got home, everything was how I left it that morning and I had to be out of my apartment by Saturday. Mike didn't want to rent a U-haul because we were moving around the corner from where I was currently staying. We used his pickup truck, and it took us almost eight hours to move and by the end of the day I was totally exhausted.

We had gotten settled in and we took a family vacation to Disney World, and we had the time of our lives, it was wonderful. Everything was going good until the phone calls started again. I was upstairs putting my daughter to bed and Mike was downstairs watching television when the phone rang.
"Is Mike there?"
"Mike has a cell phone if you want to talk to him then that's how you need to get in touch with him."
"Yeah, I heard you got a little raggedy apartment that Mike be staying at."
"Well, anything that I have is better than living in the projects." When Maureen had her baby, she had gotten on Housing and was placed in the projects. The same projects that Mike had left me stranded in when he slashed my tires. "Whoever, told you my apartment was raggedy is a hater and if you want to see for yourself, go over there and peep

that need because I don't stay there anymore. Mike and I brought us a house together."

"Yeah right."

"You think you know so much find out where it's at" and I hung up the phone.

****

I needed a drink, I thought to myself. I had, had a rough day at work and I needed to relax my mind. I dropped Mikyah off at my mom's and went to pick up Shawn. She and I were going to this new club downtown, we were riding down Market Street when I saw Mike turn the corner with a girl in his car. I couldn't make out who it was, but I knew it was a girl. I turned into an alley behind the Public Library and my timing was perfect. I pulled out right behind Mike. I followed him very closely and continued to blow my horn. He saw me and tried to lose me, but I was determined and stayed close on his tail. He stopped in the middle of the street and tried to make me run into the back of his truck, but I was able to stop my car in time. He jumped out of his truck and ran over to my car as I proceeded to get out and I saw Maureen turned around looking out of the window.

"See you still on that bull shit." He tried to smack me, but I moved, and he missed. "You can get your shit and get the fuck out. Better yet, your shit will be waiting for you in the yard. Go move in the projects with that bitch." I had put the house in my name because Mike had bad credit, so I was able to put him out without any problems. I got back into my car and closed the door. I put the car into drive, so I could pull off when he did. Mike pulled my door back open and pushed me back onto the console. We started to tussle, and I was trying to push him off me and I took my

foot off the brake and my car rolled into the back of his truck. Maureen jumped out of the truck.
"Bitch you better watch what the fuck you are doing." Shawn got out of the car, and she quickly jumped back into the truck. Mike pushed my car into park and took my keys out of the ignition he got back into his truck and left Shawn and me there. We walked down to the pay phone, but it was out of order, so we went to a BP gas station, which was closing. I waved my hands to get the young boys attention.
"We need to use the phone to call the police."
"Are you alright?"
"This guy took my keys out of my car and now I'm stranded."
"Yeah, I was watching from the window. Do you know him?"
"Unfortunately," he let us in, and we called the police.
"911 what's your emergency?" The operator asked.
"Yes, my baby's dad, Michael Mack took my keys out of my car and now I'm stranded, and my car is sitting in the middle of the street."
"Do you know where he went?"
"No."
"Well, what's his address?" I gave them his mother's address and we ended the call.

When the police arrived, they put flares around my car so no one would hit it because it was dark. The officer started walking around my car with a flashlight.
"What's the problem?"
"We contacted Mr. Mack and he said that you ran into the back of his truck and that's why he took your keys."
"That's not true. We were tussling in my car, and I had the car in drive and my foot came off the brake while I was

trying to get him off of me and my car rolled into the back of his truck." She shook her head.
"Yeah, because I see there's any damage to your vehicle." Another officer pulled up ten minutes later and gave me back my keys. I said forget about that drink that I thought I needed, I took Shawn home and I went home too.

When I got home Mike was already there. I got the baby out of the car, and we went into the house and Mike was in the bed.
"I thought I told you to get the fuck out?"
"Why are you acting like that?"
"You still trying to be with that bitch, so I'm letting you do that."
"Man, today was my son's birthday party."
"So, what, she could have found another ride there. Did she give you some gas money for taking her?"
He started laughing. "I'm not laughing. It's not funny to me."
"Come here." Mike pulled me close to him and kissed me on the forehead. "I love you baby and you don't have anything to worry about. I dropped them off and you see where I came." I forgave him as usual, and we fell asleep in each other's arms.

CHAPTER- 39

A few months prior I went to Mike's car wash and Tye was sitting there watching T.V.
"What's up Kya?"
"Hey" and I kept walking.
"So, how's the baby?"
"She's good."
"You know I just had another one too."
"For real?" I sat down to talk with her, and she and I ended up talking for a while and she wanted to call it a truce.
"So, you still got the same pager number?"
"Yup."
"Alright, I'm going to hit you up and here," she handed me a piece of paper with her phone number on it. Tye didn't care too much for Maureen because she thought she was the shit and couldn't anyone touch her and she wasn't that bright especially when it came to Mike, but neither was I. One Sunday I had worked from 6:00 am until 2 pm to get some extra hours. I had just walked into my mom's house to pick up Mikyah and I had lied on the couch while I waited for my mom to come upstairs from washing her clothes. Her phone rang. I got up and went into her room and grabbed the cordless.
"Hello?"-
"May I speak to Kya please?" It was Tye. My mom's number was listed in the phonebook, so everyone had access to it.
"What's up?"
"Nothing, what are you doing?"
"Nothing but lying on the couch, I just got off of work."
"Look, Mike is about to drop Maureen off over here to get her hair done."

"For real?" I had told Tye about the incident when Mike had taken my keys and Maureen getting out of the truck like she was bout it and calling me a bitch. "I'll be there in fifteen minutes." I got up, got Mikyah and started putting on her shoes. I already had on my jeans and tennis shoes because the weekends were dress down days.
"Mom," I called from the living room. "I'm about to go."
"Where are you going?"
"I got something to do." I stopped over my girl Doris' house to let her know what was going on, she was my partner in crime and was down for whatever.
"Aye, I need you to roll down Tye's with me."
"Why what's up?"
"Maureen is over there. Tye called me and said that Mike was about to drop her off and I don't trust her, they might be scheming to jump me." A few of Doris's friends were over there and overheard our conversation.
"I'm going too; I can't stand either one of those bitches." One of them said.
"Well, I'm rolling too because you know I got ya'll back" the other one said. We all piled into my car and went over Tye's. I saw Maureen standing in the door when I pulled up and by the time, I made my way to the door she was gone. Tye saw me walk up on her stoop and signaled for me to come in. I walked in and Doris and her girls stayed outside. Tye pointed towards the living room to let me know where Maureen was. I walked in there and Maureen grabbed her son and picked him up.
"Put him down, you want to be all big and bad when Mike is around. Show me how much of a bitch I am."
"I didn't call you a bitch."
"I heard you and so did my girl, so now you calling us liars?" Tye come get your cousin from her." She

continued to sit there. Maureen walked in the kitchen and picked up the phone.

"Tye, can I call my dad?" I ran in the kitchen and snatched the phone out of her hand.

"Naw, I'm about to use it, so now what."

"Kya, she's not going to fight you, so you might as well come on," said Doris.

I know cause she a little bitch." I hulked up a big glob of spit from deep down in my throat and I spit it in her face. I grabbed my daughter's hand and turned my back to her and walked out of the door. I knew she was going to call Mike, so I went over Doris's, which was up the street from Tye and waited for Mike to come and get her. I waited for two hours, and he never came and then I went home.

CHAPTER- 40

Mike called me over my mom's one evening because he said he had left his house keys over his mom's. "Kya can you come home; I need my bowling ball so I can go bowling?"
"Why didn't you ask me if I wanted to go?"
"It was last minute."
"Well, we can be ready."
"Naw, I don't have time to wait. I need to get on the road, but I do have something for you." I went home to find Mike sitting in the driveway with his daughter Michelle.
"Oh, is she going with you?"
"No, I still have to drop her off at home." He came in the house and gave me a hug and a kiss and put a diamond shaped heart necklace around my neck. "I'll see you on Sunday." Something didn't seem right, but I just didn't know what it was. I waited a couple of hours and then I called his cell phone.
"Hello?" he answered on the second ring.
"Why you couldn't wait for me, I don't want to be here by myself."
"I'll be back on Sunday."
"Alright, I love you."
"I love you too."

****

Tuesday evening Mike called to let me know he was on his way home from work so I could make his plate for dinner in fifteen minutes. Five minutes after I got off the phone with him my phone rang again.
"Hello."
"What are you doing?" an unfamiliar voice asked.

"Who is this?"
"This is Maureen."
"What do you want?"
"I think we should be friends."
"I don't, I don't even like you."
"Why?"
"First of all, you were fucking my man and then you got pregnant."
"That's why you don't want my son around you?"
"It's one of the reasons."
"Well, I didn't know anything about you until you had the baby and by that time, I was already pregnant."
"I was always down at the car wash. Who the fuck did you think I was?"
"One of his baby mom's."
"Did you ever see me with a kid?"
"No."
"Alright then."
"So are ya'll still together?"
"Yeah, I told you we live together."
"You don't care if he leaves for the weekend?"
"Not if he's at bowling, no."
"Well, what about last weekend?"
"What about it?"
"He took me out of town for my birthday."
"What, you went bowling with him?"
"He didn't go bowling."
"Well, he called me because he said he left his keys at his mom's and asked me if I could let him in so that he could get his bowling ball."
"His bowling ball is at your house?"
"I told you we lived together, which part of that don't you understand."

"Well, he brought me a ring for my birthday, and he took me out of town."
"What he bought you an engagement ring?"
"Yup" I smacked my lips.
"Whatever." I knew she was lying; I could tell by the way she answered.
"He just called and told me he was on his way over here."
"He just called and asked me to fix his plate because he said he was on his way home."
"Oh, he's trying to be slick. Let's set him up."
"How?"
"Come over."
"I'm on my way."
"You don't know where I live."
"In Edgewood?" Mikyah and I got dressed, put on our shoes and went to Maureen's apartment. I got there in five minutes and sure enough Mike's truck was parked in the parking lot. I pulled next to him; Mikyah and I got out and knocked on the door. She must have seen me coming up because she opened the door right away.
"Dang, you got here fast, he just went upstairs." I saw his shoes at the bottom of the steps. I looked around to be nosy and she didn't have much, I kind of felt sorry for her. I stood in the kitchen until Mike came back downstairs. He didn't see me standing there and he started putting his shoes on.
"Hi daddy" Mikyah said. He looked back and he stood there for a second stunned.
"What the fuck are you doing here? Man, get the fuck out!"
"Oh, you were on your way home right."

"Man, I said get the fuck out of here. You don't even like her so what are you doing here." He started pushing Mikyah and me out of the door.
"Mike, fuck you, I'm done. Come and get your shit and I'm not playing." I said as I walked out the door. I knew Mike always kept his keys in the console of his car. I put Mikyah in my car, opened his car door and got his keys to take my key from the ring. He saw me and started running towards me. I dropped the keys and got out of his truck.
"Run." I heard Maureen calling. Her door was a good way from the parking lot, so I had time to run around to the driver's side of my car and get in before he got to me. I put the car in reverse, pressed on the gas and tried to hit him, but he ran on the side of his truck. I sped out of the parking lot, and he threw a bottle at my car, but I had already turned the corner, so he missed.

  I went home and packed his bags, then I went to the corner store to buy a new lock but they were closed so I put two by fours between the steps and the door so he couldn't get in. He called me that night trying to explain, but I didn't want to hear it. I turned my ringer off and went to bed. He never tried to come home. I got up that next morning and I was on my way to drop Mikyah off at daycare when Mike paged me. The first one read "111-911," then "111-411-911," then "911-911-911-911." and finally my phone number followed by 911. Something told me to go home, so I followed my instincts. I turned around and went back home and Mike was standing on the steps by the side door about to go into the house. He had kicked my door in, and it was hanging on one hinge.
"Why the fuck did you do that?"
"How the fuck are you going to lock me out of my house?"

"You don't live here anymore. You pushed me and my baby out for that sorry bitch, so go live with her."
"I'm not going nowhere, and I didn't push ya'll out. You don't even like her anyways, so why were you even over her house?"
"That's not the question. Why the fuck was you over there when you had just told me you were on your way home?"
"My son was sick, and he needed some juice."
"So, you had to take off your shoes and coat to give him some juice, huh?"
"I had to use the bathroom."
"And they don't have carpet in the projects and mine is brand new and I always have to bitch about you not taking your shoes off over here."
"Whatever, man."
"Yeah, you always say that shit when I'm right. Your shit is already packed up so get it and skedaddle."
"I told you I'm not leaving."
"Okay stay. I'm calling the police." He grabbed me by my arm.
"Baby, don't do that." His whole demeanor changed. "I'm about to fix your door right now, I was just mad, and I didn't think before I reacted." I went into the house and called off from work because I wasn't leaving until my door was fixed because I knew Mike was careless and he would leave and leave my house open. It was still winter and after a half an hour of the door being opened my house was freezing. Mike had left to go buy a new door and Mikyah and I sat in front of the heater with our coats, hats and gloves on. Mike returned about an hour later with his uncle and a new door. They worked at the door for an hour and couldn't get it hung because it was too wide and long.

I left and took Mikyah to daycare so she could be warm, then I came back home and called my mom at work.
"Hey you."
"Hey baby."
"Can you do me a favor and pick up Mikyah when you get off of work?"
"Where are you?"
"At home."
"Why aren't you at work?"
"Because Mike kicked my door down when I was on my way, something just told me to come back home."
"I am so sick of him. Is your dad at home?"
"I don't know."
"Did he fix your door?"
"He's trying, but he can't get it on."
"Well, I'm about to call your dad." We hung up and twenty minutes later my dad pulled into my driveway. He must have told Mike to leave because when I looked out of the window, he was going down the street. My dad came in the house and up the stairs.
"Kya."
"Yeah?"
"Come in here." I went into the kitchen.
"So why did he kick your door in?" I found myself always trying to defend him.
"I told him he had to get out and I locked him out, but he brought another door."
"I'm not putting that door up there. I'll go buy you a steel door, that wood is not an outside door." We sat and talked until my mom arrived at 3:00 pm. She and my dad went to the store and brought a new door, and had it hung and had put the wood door at the top of the steps that lead to my

kitchen by 6 pm. Just in time for me to pick Mikyah up from daycare.

When my dad fixed my door, he put the same locks on the door and when I came home from work the next day, Mike had dinner cooked and Mikyah's clothes out and ironed for the next day. I still had an attitude, and I didn't want him there. I went straight to the bathroom and got washed up. He was sitting on the couch watching television and when I came back downstairs, he had our plates made and he and Mikyah were sitting at the table. "Are you going to eat with us?" I didn't answer, I just sat down at the table and ate the steak and macaroni and cheese he had made. After we ate, I washed the dishes, took a bath and got my baby and myself ready for bed. I stayed in my room until I fell asleep. The next day I went down to the University and registered for classes to pursue my career. Every evening until classes started, I would go to my mom's house to eat dinner and I would stay until around 8 or 9 pm and by the time I got home it was time to go to bed. After a week of the same routine, I guess Mike got the clue because he stopped coming over and the last time we were there at the same time, I had taken my house key from his key ring, so he no longer had a key to my house.

That following evening Mike came over and realized his key was missing from his key ring when he tried to come into the house, and he began to bang on my door.
"What?" I asked through the closed door.
"Open the door."
"No, you need to leave."
"You got some nigga up in there don't you?"

"Nope, I'm in the bed."
"Open this damn door or you'll wish you had of."
"Whatever. You better leave before I call the police."
"Fuck the police. I'm going to give you a reason to call them" and he walked away from the door and got back into his truck. I had brought a new truck so I had my car off to the side of the yard and my truck in the backyard, just in case one didn't start I wouldn't have myself blocked in. Mike rammed his truck into the back of my truck and my alarm went off, then he called me from his cell phone.
"You still not gon' open the door?"
"Nope, but I called the police and they're on their way" I hadn't for real, but I just told him that. He backed his truck up and rammed it into the back of my car now both of my alarms were going off. He then peeled out of my driveway and sped down the street. The next morning, I went outside to see the damage. My bumper was bent on my truck and my headlight was busted out on my car. I went into the house and called the police, and they came out and took a police report and after they left, I called Mike.
"I just wanted to tell you that you might have a warrant for your arrest because I called the police and made a police report."
"Why the fuck did you do that shit? I was going to fix it."
"Well, you shouldn't have done it. I'm tired of you tearing up my shit." He hung up on me. Monday morning, he had the part to fix my headlight and he put it on but my bumper on my truck was still bent, but I still dropped the charges.

CHAPTER- 41

It was the beginning of May, and my Aunt Jasman had her fortieth birthday party. Everyone closes to her were to bring a covered dish because she had invited over one hundred and fifty people. I had Tye make the baked beans that I was supposed to prepare because she liked to cook, and she didn't mind. I dropped them off because there were no kids allowed at her party and my mom was out of town but was expected back later that evening and I didn't allow just anyone to watch my daughter. I asked my aunt to put me a plate up and told her I'd be back later. Her party was planned to start at 6 pm and by 8:30 I had grown impatient. I was sitting on the couch all dressed in a Nautica jean outfit, and my brand-new Jordan's, when my mom called and told me she was on her way to get the baby. I put her jacket on and made sure she had everything she wanted to take with her because I wasn't planning on getting her until the next day. When my mom came, I walked out the door with her, got into my car and went to the party.

When I arrived at the party everyone began to greet me like I was a celebrity.
"Hey Kya."
"Where you been?"
"How's the baby?"
"Are you hungry?" Questions were coming at me in all directions. I felt good because I know they had missed my presents. I looked at the food and it was just about all gone.
"Aye, where's my plate?"
"It's in the refrigerator."

"Alright." I gave everyone a hug, and then headed to the refrigerator to get my plate because I was starving.
"Dang, excuse me. Where you been all night?" A very nice-looking guy said.
"At home sleep."
"Why you worked all day?"
"Not today, but I do work, go to school and I'm a single mom. I try to get my rest when I can."
"I hear you. Why don't you come dance with me?"
"I'm about to eat."
"Come on this is my song, just one dance." Brother was fine. He was light skinned, my type of brother, tall, with naturally curly hair.
"Okay, just for you," I said with q smile. He grabbed my hand and led me down the basement where the DJ was, and we danced to "*Peaches and Cream*" by 112 and then we sat down on the couch.
"So, what did you say your name was?"
"I didn't" and I smiled "but its Kya."
"You have some beautiful teeth."
"Thank you and your name is?"
"Thomas." We shook hands.
"Well Thomas, I don't want to cut you short or be rude, but a sister is hungry."
"That's cool. It was nice meeting you." I went upstairs and got my plate from the refrigerator. Just as I was taking my food out of the microwave, I heard Thomas saying his good-byes."
"You're leaving so soon?" I asked.
"Yeah, I was like one of the first people here."
"Oh" and I shrugged my shoulders and started eating my food.

"Why don't you walk me outside?" I grabbed a plastic fork and followed him outside.
"So how long have you been in school?"
"Five years. I already have a degree in Computer Programming and now I'm working on my Business Management Degree."
"For real? That's good."
"How much longer do you have to go?"
"I have about eight more classes, so about a year." He shook his head.
"That's alright."
"So, what do you do for a living?"
"I just drive a train."
"Just... man that sounds exciting."
"It's alright. So why don't you give me your number and we can finish this conversation later because I know your food is getting cold." I had forgotten all about my food.
"How old are you first."
"Thirty-one."
"Alright, well why don't you give me your number?"
"I want to make sure I hear from you so give me yours and you'll get mine when I call you." I had to laugh because that was one of my lines. I felt a vibe between us, so I gave him my home phone number, something I never gave out. He seemed like someone special, and I followed my instincts, and I went back to the party.
"Where you been all this time?" My aunt asked.
"Conversating."
"To that little cutie that was here?" I tilted my head and popped my collar as I laughed.
"You know."
"Almost everybody in here was trying to get with him all night."

"Well, everybody's not me." One of her girls turned her nose up at me and smacked her lips. I laughed and walked into the living room where my cousins and other aunts were taking pictures and giving my aunt Jasman messages on the camcorder. It was always funny when broads hated on me and that was one of the main reasons why I didn't hang around a bunch of females. If you weren't my friend from back in the day, then a friend to me you would never be.

CHAPTER- 42

Thomas and I had really become close. He was what I was missing in my life. He called me everyday to see how my day was and we'd talk for hours even though he was at work. He always made time for me and that meant a lot. On his days off we would go shoot pool and have a couple of drinks or just chill and watch a movie. I had told him almost everything that Mike had put me through, and I let him know that I was afraid of commitment and we both agreed to take things slow. Two months had gone by and one evening he got off early and came over to watch a movie. He had never pushed up on me and I respected him for that. He had brought a six-pack of Corona and I had a fifth of Tarantula, which was blue tequila. We drank half of the six-pack and half of the tequila and then I put in the movie "*Love and Basketball*". I had on a pair of daisy dukes and a jersey because it was really hot that day.

"Man, it's hot in here. Do you have another jersey I can put on?" I turned on the ceiling fan.

"I'm not about to go back upstairs, my daughter's asleep."

"Well do you mind if I get comfortable?"

"I don't care." He unbuttoned his shirt and took off his shoes and socks, lied on the couch and pulled me on top of him. We lied there, watched the movie and then he kissed me on the forehead, then on my nose and I moved up and kissed him on the lips. He began to kiss me very passionately and rubbing his fingers through my hair and it was feeling so good. I couldn't remember the last time anyone had made me feel this way.

"Oh Thomas" I moaned. He put his hands up my shirt and caressed my back and then he unbuttoned my bra as he

moaned my name. From that kiss I knew I was in love, and I never wanted that feeling to end. I was rubbing my fingers through his naturally curly hair when I heard a car door shut outside in my driveway. It was late and no one came over my house unannounced, so I got up and looked out of the window and I saw Mike's truck in the driveway. Although I hadn't seen nor really talked to Mike in a couple of weeks, I figured he realized I was serious about it being over, but when I saw his car, I panicked. I gasped for air and my eyes got big.
"Put your shoes on." Thomas just sat up and looked at me like I was crazy. "My baby's dad is here." I heard my screen door pop open, which meant that he had pulled it hard enough to pop the lock. I hurriedly fixed my bra, and I heard the side door open. I opened the door at the top of the steps and Mike was standing there. He must have had an extra key somewhere. I stood there and he walked up the stairs casually and moved me out of his way. I was in shock and didn't know what to do.
"Oh, so this is what it is? Man, why the fuck are you sitting up here chilling with my woman?" Mike picked up a beer bottle and started walking toward Thomas and I tried to grab it out of his hand because it was my fight and Thomas didn't have anything to do with it. Mike and I started tussling and ended up in the dining room. We had knocked the table and the chairs over and I asked Thomas to leave because I knew Mike wasn't going to and if he did, he would have done something to his car or something else stupid. I could have called the police but I figured I had already fucked up and Mike had already been in trouble with the law so many times and I didn't want to see him locked up because he would probably get five years if he went back to jail. I stood in the door and watched Thomas

pull off and I wished I had handled that situation better. Mike pulled back into the driveway after letting Thomas out and came into the house and the phone rang. I tried to grab it, but he pushed me out of the way and picked it up. "Hello? Man, this is my woman and don't call her anymore" and he hung up the phone.
"So, you were in here fucking that yellow nigga? Where is my daughter?"
"She's in the bed." He grabbed me by my shirt and pulled me up the stairs. I picked up the phone to call the police, but he smacked the phone out of my hand and when it hit the floor it rang.
"Answer it and tell that nigga don't call you anymore." I answered the phone, and it was Thomas.
"I hope you get what you deserve" and he hung up on me and I broke down in tears. I hated Mike, he always went in the streets and did what he wanted to do but tried to put my life on hold. We weren't even together anymore, but yet, he was still running my life. He pushed me on the bed and started trying to take off my shorts and I was pushing him away.
"You were in here watching a porno and fucking that nigga, that's why you don't want to give me none?"
"I'm not your woman." He put his hands around my neck and started chocking me.
"You are my woman and I love you and I will kill you and anybody that try to take you away from me." I just laid there as tears flowed down my face. He let my neck go and pulled down my shorts and I crossed my legs at the ankles so he couldn't get them off, but he managed too anyway. I still had on my panties, and I was holding on to them with my life and he just ripped them in half. He tried to put my legs over my shoulders so he could enter me but I made my

legs stiff so he couldn't. He put his hands between my thighs and tried to pry my legs open, but he couldn't so he uncrossed my feet and pulled me to the middle of the bed by my legs and pushed my legs over my shoulders and penetrated me. I tried to push him away, but I couldn't, so I just lay there while he drilled me hard.
"You better not ever give my pussy away. You're my woman and I want us to be a family and have another baby." I closed my eyes tight to try to stop the tears from falling. When he was finished, I tried to get up so I could go downstairs to sleep on the couch since he wouldn't leave.
"Where are you going?"
"Downstairs, I need to get something." He put his leg over my legs and his arm across my chest, so I couldn't get up. I laid there staring at the ceiling until I cried myself to sleep.

****

I had gotten a prepaid cell phone, since I was not eligible for a contract because I had gotten a phone in my name for Mike while he was in the Oriana house, and he ran the bill up. I didn't have long distance on my house phone and Thomas had a Cleveland phone number and that was the only way I could call him, and I was not about to let him get away. I called the phone company that next day and had them add long distance to my phone and I got one hundred free minutes and three cents a minute after that. This was a price I was willing to pay to get him back into my life. I called him on my way to work and the call went straight to voicemail, which meant he had his phone turned off. I wanted to call off from work, but I had not too long ago started a new job in my field of study, and it offered good pay and benefits, and I was still in my probationary period. I couldn't afford to lose my job over a man. I sat at my desk and cried all day. My arm had whelps all over it from the tussle Mike and I had. I called Thomas on every one of my breaks, but it continued to go to voicemail. Mike come over that evening and every evening for the next couple of days and I ignored his presents because I felt that he didn't want me, but he did want anyone else to have me either and it wasn't fair. Thomas was the first person that I had falling in love with since I had met Mike Seven years ago and he was the only person that made me realize that I was a good woman, I had a lot going for myself and I didn't have to settle. Everything he said I already knew and everyone else had tried to tell me, but I was blinded by love, and I needed him to shine a light on the bigger picture. I had met a lot of people during our relationship, but no one had ever had the power to make me want to leave Mike. I believe Thomas was sent from heaven and that's why I felt it was so important to make mends with him. After three days of continuous calling Thomas finally answered the phone. I had left him several messages, but he never returned any of my calls. When he answered the phone, it shocked me because I had already prepared my speech for his voicemail.

"Hello?" Just hearing his voice brought a smile to my face.
"Hey what's up?"
"Nothing. Who is this?" That kind of hurt my feelings because I knew he knew my voice.
"This is Kya. Dang, you forgot about me?"
"Naw, what's up?"
"I feel I owe you an apology. I handled that situation wrong and I'm sorry. I'm not trying to lose you; you are something special to me. I never believed in love at first sight until I met you."

"Well, you should have thought about all of that before you played me like you did. You put me in a messed-up situation, and I didn't appreciate it, that's how people get killed. I told you what I went through with the last girl I was with, and I don't have time for this drama." His last girl had given him a key to her place, and he walked in on her and another man in bed together.
"I know that's why I keep calling you apologizing because I know I messed up and I regret the decision I made everyday."
"Why didn't you call me when he left and tell me to come back?"
"Because I couldn't get him to leave."
"See that's what I'm talking about. He has too much control over your life and until you get your shit together, you're always going to be miserable." Tears begin to fill my eyes because he was right.
"Thomas."
"You have a good life" and he hung up in my face. I felt my heart shatter in a thousand pieces. I sat on my stairs and cried for a good half an hour. I had never been a quitter at anything that I felt so strongly about, and I was destined to get him back.

    I gave Thomas a couple of days to calm down before I called him back. The first couple of times he said he was busy, and he would call me back and he never did, so I would call him back and finally he talked to me, and we made up. We weren't boyfriend and girlfriend, but I didn't care, as long as I had apart of him. Mike called and told me he was moving to California and that I could go ahead and "do me". After six months of whining, begging and pleading I finally got Thomas to come over and he spent the night with me, and everything was going good with us until one Sunday. It was Mikyah's fourth birthday and Mike called me.

"What are you doing?"

"Watching TV."

"Do you miss me?" I got quiet. "Well, I miss you. Did my baby have a good birthday?"

"Yeah, she had a good time at Chuck E. Cheese's."

"That's good. Where is she?"

"Upstairs in her room."

"Well tell her that I'm sorry I didn't make it to her party, but I got her something nice."

"I'm sure she'll appreciate it."

"Well open the door so I can give it to her." I looked out of the window and his car was parked in my driveway and he was getting out of his car.

"Fuck." I said to myself. I wasn't ready for him to come back. I opened the door, and he brought her new big girl bike into the house.

"Mikyah" I called. I heard her little feet run across the floor upstairs. Mike hugged me but I just stood there.

"I missed you baby." I pushed him away from me.

"Daddy" Mikyah ran and jumped in her daddy's arms. He hugged and kissed her.

"I missed you baby."

"I missed you too daddy."

"You see what I bought you for your birthday."

"That's too big."

"Because you're getting to be a big girl," I went into the kitchen to let them have their time. He came into the kitchen a few minutes later and we talked until about 10 pm.

"Well, I'm about to go to bed."

"Come on."
"No, you have to leave." He gave me a hurt look.
"You haven't seen me in two months." I turned my head.
He kissed me on my lips and left. I didn't want Mike anywhere around me. I wanted things between Thomas and me to work out and I knew that Mike would make that impossible.

CHAPTER- 43

I wouldn't say Thomas and I were boyfriend and girlfriend, but we were more that friends. He'd come over on his days off, he made sure we talked every day, and he was finally comfortable at my house, but he was afraid to commit to me. A couple of months had gone by, and he started working a lot of over time, he had started his own lawn company and his time with me became limited and I started to get bored. On my birthday he had to work, and he usually didn't get off until 2 am. Mike called and asked if he could take me to dinner. I didn't have anything else to do, so I took him up on his offer. We went to the Outback Steak house and had a wonderful time. I still had feelings for Mike, but I really didn't want to be with him, but I didn't want anyone else to have him either. He started calling me again on a regular basis. We went to the movies, to the IX center and started doing everything like we use to. He had given up his place when he went to California, so he was staying here and there, but mainly with his mom.
"Kya, why don't you let me come home? I promise you things will be better. I want us to be a family."
"Naw, I don't think that's best, we've tried that before and it didn't work."
"I've grown up and I've seen all the mistakes I've made, and I want to make it up to you. I'll pay half of the mortgage and half of the utilities and do what ever needs to be done around the house." I was kind of struggling and I could use the help. We had been getting along pretty well and we hadn't been arguing or anything.
"Alright, but this is our last try, if this don't work then it's not meant for us to be together."
"It's going to work, you'll see."

The first year was great. He took the baby to daycare every morning, so she could sleep in, he picked her up and he even babysat while I went to the club with my girls. On my late nights he would have dinner ready, and the dishes washed when I got home. He made sure Mikyah, and my clothes were ironed for the next day, he was acting like we were really married, and we hardly ever argued. He gave me one thousand dollars the first month he was there and told me to take what I needed. I didn't try to take advantage of him, and I only took what we agreed upon. Summer rolled around and once again things started changing for the worst. Mike stopped coming home at night or he'd wait until I went to sleep and then he would leave and when I asked him where he'd been, he'd always say working. Mike and I had both started sleeping and eating a lot. We noticed it about each other, but not about ourselves. That following month I missed my period.
"Mike, I think I'm pregnant."
"Whatever."
"I'm serious."
"Okay." I wasn't about to argue with him about it, so we went on with our everyday lives. One night we were making love and I was rubbing on his back when I felt all these scratches. I pushed him up and turned on the bed light.
"What are you doing?" I looked on his back and where the scratches were, he couldn't have done them himself.
"What happened to your back?"
"What are you talking about?"
"All of these scratches." I traced them with my finger.
"I must have been itching."
"You can't even reach down here." He tried to feel them.

"Man, you're tripping."
"Whatever." Now I had my eye open on his every move. I was cleaning the house one afternoon, and I found a receipt. I looked at it to make sure it wasn't anything important before I threw it away. The receipt contained a pack of diapers and a can of Similac, and the purchase was made with Mike's debit card. I put the receipt on the dining room table so he would see it when he came home and to give him a few minutes to get his lie together. When I heard him pull in the driveway, I went in the living room and sat down on the couch so that I could see him walk through the dining room. He sat down at the table to take off his shoes and I saw him glance at the receipt out of the corner of his eye. I went into the dining room and pushed the receipt into his lap.
"So, who are you buying simalic and diapers for?"
"That's my brother's."
"So, your brother used your debit card?"
"Since you all in my business, he didn't have any money, so he asked me to get it for him and he paid me when I took him home."
"Okay, let the truth be told" and I walked away. Now I was always on alert.
"Kya, I need to talk to you anyways."
"What's up?"
"I'm about to get Mikel for the summer because his mom in on something else."
"I told you that bitch was sorry."
"I don't want to hear that."
"Well, if you're asking me can he stay here then you already know the answer."
"So, what am I supposed to do?"

"Let his mother raise him like most moms do. She shouldn't have had him if she couldn't take care of him. I have a child and one on the way I don't need any extra responsibilities."
"It won't be your responsibility, it'll be mine."
"I can't do it, I'm sorry."
"Well, I got to take care of mine, so I gotta do what I gotta do."
"Whatever." He took a shower and got dressed and left and didn't come back that night.

  When Mike moved in, to show me that he was being totally faithful and that he had nothing to hide, he had given me the access code to his voicemail and I never used it, but I knew he was up to no good, so I utilized my resources. The first couple of times I called there were no messages, so I started calling at five and six o'clock in the morning on the nights he didn't make it home and one morning I got lucky. There was a girl on his voicemail that sounded a little hostile.
"Mike, you need to take care of your son, I'm tired of doing this alone. He needs some new shoes. You can let that bitch of yours keep you away from him if you want to." I skipped the message so he could still hear it. I paged him "911" and he called right back and the name on the caller ID read "Mona Strickland." I knew he wouldn't be dumb enough to call me from another girl's house without blocking out the number, so I figured that must have been one of his boy's houses who lived with their girlfriend.
"So, you supposed to have had another baby?"
"Now what are you talking about?"
"Just what I said" he smacked his lips.
"No, is that all you called me for?"

"Why are you not here?"
"I gotta get my shit right so I can take care of my son."
"Yeah right." That following weekend I went to the hood Internet to see what the word on the street was and I heard several different stories and none of them were the same. I just said forget it I would just wait it out, the truth was bound to come out, and it always does. For the next couple of days every time I paged Mike, he'd call me back from the same number. This time I wasn't really hurt, that meant it wasn't true or I really didn't care anymore. Mike hadn't come home for almost a week, and I hadn't called him, but he was holding up my life, so I called him to see where we stood.
"What, you moved out?"
"I told you I was getting my son. We've been staying with my mom."
"Well, if you're going to be here then you need to be here, if not then get your stuff out so I can go on with my life."
"You know what… I'm tired of you telling me to leave. I'm coming to get my shit and you don't ever have to worry about me coming back to that bitch." He got to my house in ten minutes with four of his kids in the car. He packed everything that could fit in his car.
"I'll send my pops to get my dresser and my bike."
"What are we going to do about this baby? I'm not about to raise two kids by myself." He looked at me, rolled his eyes, got into his car and left. I was kind of hurt but at the same time I was relieved. I didn't want to raise two kids by myself because I was already struggling, but they say that God will never give you more than you can handle. Mike called every now and then to see how we were doing, but I had gotten so stressed out with him, his son, this new

situation with Mona, my job and everyday life that I lost the baby.

    I got to work a little late because I was trying to get in touch with Mike because I had been bleeding for the past two weeks. I had called the doctor, but he was booked for the next two weeks. I went to work and around 4:30 our company president called me into the conference room. I had written him a letter a month prior asking him about a raise he had promised me that I had never received. He told me that do to the contract he was unable to grant my request. I kept feeling a lot of pressure in the bottom of my stomach. I went to get Mikyah from daycare so I could go home and lie down. When I got out of my truck, I felt something heavy drop and it was pressing down on the inside of my vagina. I went inside the building and got my baby and hurried home. I went upstairs to use the bathroom because it felt like I had to urine and when I went to relieve myself more than pee came out. My undeveloped baby fell into the toilet. I stood there with my pants still to my ankles and stared at it. I wanted to get it out, but it looked disgusting. I washed my hands and went into my bedroom and called Mike's cell phone, but it was disconnected so I paged him 911 and by this time I was really crying. Surprisingly he called me back before I could walk out of my room.
"I need you to get over here."
"What's wrong?"
"Could you just come on?"
"I'll be there in a minute." I went back downstairs and lay on the couch and ten minutes later I heard Mike pull in the driveway. I met him at the side door. He walked it the house looking distraught.

"Come here." I headed upstairs to the bathroom, and he followed me. I opened the toilet seat.
"Look."
"What's that?"
"Our baby" he looked at me like I was crazy, then he looked back into the toilet and just stared at the undeveloped fetus.
"Go get something to put it in." I went downstairs and looked through the cabinet until I found an old butter container and a lid and took it back upstairs and gave it to Mike, who was still staring in the toilet. I then went into my room to change my clothes. I heard the water swishing around in the toilet.
"Ugh." I heard Mike yell. He was trying to get the fetus out of the toilet. I started laughing inside and some how that made me feel a little better. I wasn't that hurt because I really didn't want another baby by Mike because he had too many kids already and Mikyah was older now and it was easier to find a babysitter. Mike's family really didn't help me out with our baby, and it wasn't their responsibility, so I depended a lot on my family. Mike came out of the bathroom.
"Come on."
"Where are we going?"
"To the hospital" I sighed because I hated hospitals, but I knew Mike would make me go, so I just put my shoes on while he got Mikyah ready.

When we arrived at the hospital, we ended up having to wait four hours before I was able to see a doctor because it was so crowded and by that time I was beginning to cramp very badly and Mikyah had become hungry, impatient and restless. Mike had left his wallet at home,

and I only had two dollars and some change, so we put our change together to get us some snacks out of the vending machine. Mike had gotten a cup of coffee and we went outside because it was hurting for me to sit.
"Kya Walters" I heard the receptionist call over the loudspeaker. We went back inside the hospital and followed the doctor to the little room.
"Get undressed and put on this gown." I did what I was told and lied down on the bed while Mike and Mikyah sat in a chair by the door.
"Ya'll can go wait in the lobby."
"No, we're staying right here." I believe Mike thought I was faking, and he wanted to hear everything the doctor had to say. The doctor came back in and checked me to make sure everything was intact, and he wrote me a prescription for pain pills.
"Here" Mike stood up and handed the doctor the container that was beginning to smell bad. "This came out of her when she went to the bathroom."
"What is it?"
"We don't know. You're the doctor."
"Here, I'll take it to the lab and get it checked." He took the container and left. I got dressed and we waited another half an hour. By this time Mikyah was asleep in her daddy's arms. The doctor returned.
"Yes, that was the embryo, it was about eights weeks." We went home, Mike made us dinner and we went to bed. I was from work for the next three days and the next day was terrible. I was hurting so badly, and Mike was at work and took his sweet time bringing me my pain pills. I had paged him all morning and finally he brought my pills. *I'm so glad I don't have to deal with this shit on a regular basis.* I thought.

CHAPTER- 44

"Kya are you and my baby going to come over and spend the night with me in my new house?"
"Oh, you finally got on your feet?"
"Yeah, you know me I only be down for a minute." My losing the baby had really brought Mike and I close again, we weren't a couple, but we did everything that couples did. Mikyah and I stayed most of the weekend with Mike and he periodically stayed with us, and I even let Mikel stay with him. One Thursday Mikyah and I stayed with Mike because she was now in the kindergarten and her school was closed that Friday and I had to work, and Mike agreed to watch her. We were lying in the living room watching a movie when someone blew their horn in Mike's driveway.
"I'll be right back."
"You're supposed to be spending time with us. Where are you going?"
"I'll be right back." Mike left and by 10 pm I was ready to go to bed, but Mike hadn't returned. I paged him and called his cell phone, and he didn't answer or returned my call, so I text him.
"*Baby I'm ready to go to bed, so come home.*" He still didn't call me back nor come home so I went to bed. By midnight I was sound asleep when I heard someone banging on his front door.
"Kya, it's me, open the door." I looked out the peephole and it was Mrs. Mack. I opened the door and let her in.
"You might want to go home."
"Why where's Mike?"
"The police beat him up pretty badly and now he's in jail and can't make anymore phone calls." There was nothing I

could do, so I got Mikyah up and we went home, and I called Cleo to see if he could watch Mikyah while I went to work the next day.

That evening I was walking in the door to pick Mikyah up from Cleo's when my cell phone rang.
"Hello?"
"Kya."
"What's up?"
"Where you at?"
"Picking up Mikyah."
"Can you come and get me?"
"Where are you?"
"Walking down Grant. When they said I was free to go, I just started walking. I was just glad to be out of that place."
"Alright I'm on my way." When I pulled up Mike was walking with his head down looking at the ground, he looked pitiful. He got into the car, and I saw a big knot on the back of his head. He looked at me and tears filled his eyes.
"I never should have left." When he started to talk, I noticed all the gold in his mouth was gone and his tooth was chipped and loose. His shirt was dusty, and he had dried up blood on it. He looked a mess.
"What happened?"
"They tried to set me up. I shook hands with my dude, and they said I gave him some drugs, and then all these police cars swooped up on me. They put a gun to my head and told me to get on the ground, I did, and they cuffed me and the same officer that arrested me the last time kicked me in the mouth and said that this time I wasn't getting off so easily and that they should take me in an alley and kill me.

See…" He showed me his teeth. "They knocked my gold off of my teeth with them hard ass boots and my tooth is loose." I didn't comment I just shook my head because Mike was always in a bunch of nonsense. We went to his mom's so he could tell her what happened. We sat there for an hour or so and then I had to go get my hair done so I left.
"Kya, are you going to stay the night with me?"
"We'll see."
"Well call me when you get finished." I didn't feel comfortable staying at his house with everything that was going on with him so when I was finished getting my hair done, I went and picked him up and he stayed the weekend with me.

The following week I took a vacation so that I could take care of Mike. I took him to the dentist, we went to the prosecutor's office to press charges on the officer, got all his paperwork together, talked to a couple of lawyers and spent some quality time together. After ten days he was back to his old self.
"My leg is still a little sore but I'm going to go bowling this weekend."
"You need to get away for a minute to sort your thoughts."
"I'll be back Sunday night, so I'll talk to you later." Mike left and I went home to enjoy the weekend to myself.

"Kya, you sleep?"
"No, I'm just lying here." It was 8:30 Sunday morning.
"Girl, let me tell you what happened, and you didn't hear this from me."
"What's up?"
"Last night Mike punched Mona in the mouth at the club."

"I thought he was at bowling."
"I don't know but he had this F-150, it looked kind of new, and he and Mona were in the club together and they got into it and when they got outside, she was all in his face talking boss and he punched her in her shit. He dropped her like a nigga, and she fell to the ground."
"For real?"
"He called Tye and her sister over his house to whip her ass because she had busted out his window, but she wouldn't fight them."
"Um, well let me call over there and see what happened."
"Don't put my name in it."
"Come on man, you know me better than that." I hung up the phone and called Mike, but I got his voicemail, so I paged him. I waited ten minutes for him to return my call then Mikyah and I got dressed and went to his house. When I pulled up there were two police cars sitting on the street. I didn't see Mike's car, but I got out and knocked on the door anyways because I was trying to see if he was in the police car or if they would give me some information as to what was going on. I didn't get anywhere with the officers, so I went to his mom's house.
"Mrs. Mack, did you see those police cars in front of Mike's house?"
"Yeah, what's going on?"
"I don't know. I knocked on the door, but he didn't answer so he must be in some kind of trouble."
"I don't know." She called him at home, and he didn't answer, then she unblocked her number and called his cell phone and he answered.
"Why are all those police cars sitting in front of your house? What? I thought you were supposed to be bowling.

Um, well Kya over here, she's worried about you." She handed me the phone.
"When did you get back?"
"Last night, why?"
"Did you have fun at the club?"
"I don't have time for this bull shit." That was the first sign of guilt.
"Well, I'm going to bring you the rest of your things, because I don't have time for it either."
"Don't come over here because I'm not going to let you in."
"I don't need to come in."
"Put my mom back on the phone and get from over there." I handed his mom the phone and sat there until she was done talking. We talked for a while then Mike called her back and she handed me the phone.
"I told you to get the fuck away from my mom's house."
"Okay bye" and I hung up the phone. I got up to leave and he was standing outside.
"Quit coming around here."
"Remember you said it, I didn't."
"Fuck you bitch!"
"What you mad at me for? I didn't call the police on you for punching me in the face. You need to be mad at your new baby mama."
"That's not my fucking baby mama" and he started coming towards my car. I started laughing as I got into my truck and pulled off. I rolled down my window.
"I'll be back in ten minutes with your stuff, and I'll have my brother bring your dresser and stuff over, so you don't have to make a trip."
"Don't come over here or send nobody over my house because I'm not going to answer the door." I rolled my

window up and pulled off. I went home and packed up the rest of his clothes that he had left when he had taken his things a few months earlier. I parked around the corner so the police wouldn't see my car if they came back, and Mikyah and I walked over there with his bags. When I had ridden past his front door was opened, but by the time I walked around the corner it was closed again. I went through the fence and went to the back door, and I knocked, but he didn't answer. I looked up and his window was broken, so my resources knew what they were talking about. I put his clothes on the back porch, went home, finished my baby's hair and went to spend the day with my mom.

****

Monday morning, I was sitting at my desk thinking how I didn't want to be involved in a relationship because it was too much trouble and drama involved and how I was happy by myself. I was kind of struggling with my bills, but I'd rather struggle than be miserable, then my phone vibrated in my pocked. I looked at it and I had a new text message. I read it and it said: "*I love you*" it was from Mike. I texted him back. "*You're a liar and I hate liars.*" He replied: "*I've been going through a lot. We need to talk, call me when you get off.*" I was interested in what he had to say, so I called him when I got off.
"Kya, look I need somewhere to go, the police have been over here three times and they've been by my aunt's and by my mom's, twice."
"Go stay with your new girlfriend."
"You are my girlfriend."
"No, I'm not."
"Well could you come and get me on your way home?" I don't know why I felt obligated, and I always felt sorry for

him even though he always did me wrong. I went over there and picked him up.
"Just give me a week to get my money right and I'll turn myself in."
"Well, I'm going to let you know out the gate, I have a friend that calls me, he's not my boyfriend, we're just good friends. Someone I can talk to."
"You can talk to me."
"Not about everything, I can't." We rode to my house in silence and that Thursday Mike turned himself in. He ended up getting six more months in the Oriana house. I went to visit him once, but when I found out Mona was coming to visit him, I never came back because I had flashbacks about what had happened with Angelica. Mike came over when he was allowed out on Saturdays and Sundays, and I would take him back some evenings if I didn't have anything else to do. I had really lost interest in Mike, and I had made a stern choice that I was going on with my life. My daughter was old enough to understand and I would still let her see her daddy whenever she wanted. I was tired of Mike bringing these different women into our relationship. I was tired of him putting his hands on me and I was tired of him running my life. They say it's a thin line between love and hate and I'm a firm believer. I had met three or four new guys that I made very clear with that I didn't want a relationship, that I just wanted to be friends, and I don't sleep with my friends. I had run into a guy that I thought I was in love with when I was sixteen and I called him whenever I needed a tune up. I started hanging in the clubs and partying a lot, so my time was always occupied and during the six months Mike was gone I felt like I had a life again. I had started a new life and I was totally happy. I knew that most of the time, when you meet a guy in the

club usually all they want to do is get in your panties, but I wasn't giving up any, so they just showed me that they were really interested or willing to wait. Every time I went out everyone showed me much respect because no one could say that they slept with me and that made me feel good. A lot of girls said that I thought I was the shit, and I did because if you don't think anything of yourself then why should anyone else so that was something that they had to deal with on their own. As long as they didn't say anything to me, everything was cool.

      When Mike came home six months later, I was a totally new person and nothing he could do or say could persuade me into coming back to him. For my birthday he came to my job and brought me roses and took me to lunch and that evening he took me to dinner.
"Kya, do you want to go to the movies?"
"No, I have something to do so let me go over Tye's and get my hair braided." My friend Armani had given me some money to get my hair done. I had men Armani several months prior and we had been spending a lot of time together. Armani called me just as Tye was finishing up my hair.
"Are you ready?" Armani and I had plans to go to the hot tub club to relax, he had a lot of drama in his life and we both needed an outlet.
"Give me twenty minutes." I dropped Mikyah off at the babysitters and I rushed home, took a quick shower and put on my bikini under my jeans and a sweater. Just as I was putting on my shoes, Armani called from the driveway.
"I'm outside."
"Here I come." I went outside and got into his car. Man, I loved this ride he had mirror tint on the windows and

twenty-inch vogues on the tires, costumed seats, a DVD player, a seven-inch TV screen and a booming system. If I were the same gold digging broad that I used to be, I probably would have fucked him just because of his car, because that was a sign of big money, but that was my homeboy. He was in my corner one hundred percent and was always there when I needed to talk and that was what I needed at the time, a good friend who didn't judge me, but kept it real. He took me to one of his apartments so he could get some money and then he left and had me sit there while he went to take care of some business and went to his house because his baby's mama had called him three times while I was in the car. He came back a half an hour later and was ready to hit the road.
"You got the directions?"
"Yeah" I went into my purse, pulled out the directions and told him which way to go. My office secretary had given me good directions. When we arrived, we had eight different rooms to pick from and they were all thirty dollars an hour. We picked the mirror room. We tuned the radio to 93.1 because it was time for the quiet storm, for lovers only where they played slow relaxing songs. We got into the hot tub with our swimming suits on and talked and laughed for the whole hour. I really enjoyed spending time with Armani. He was a good friend. When I looked at my pager after I got dressed, I had six missed calls, and they were all from Mike. I cleared them out because he wasn't about to ruin my evening.
"Could you do me a favor and pick Mikyah up from the babysitters for me?" I asked Armani.
"Where is that?"
"She's on the way." He picked her up and dropped us off at home. His pager kept going off and his cell phone kept

ringing so I figured his woman must have wanted him home, so we ended our evening. As soon as I walked in the door my phone rang, I thought it was Armani calling to tell me he had a good time, so I ran into the living room and answered the phone.
"So that's your new boyfriend?"
"Mike, what are you talking about?"
"I saw that nigga drop you and my baby off. So where did he take ya'll?"
"He didn't take us anywhere; he took me somewhere and I asked him to pick her up, so I didn't have to go back out."
"I see how you want to play, put my baby on the phone. I turned the volume up on the phone and handed it to Mikyah.
"Hi baby."
"Hi daddy."
"Where have you been?"
"Over my Aunt Jasman's."
"Who was that man that brought ya'll home?" She looked up at me.
"I don't know." He always tried to put her in the middle of grown people's business.
"Is that mommy's boyfriend?" I took the phone from her.
"Don't be giving my daughter the third degree."
"Fuck you Kya!"
"Don't you wish you could?" he hung up the phone. The next day Armani gave me some money to buy an outfit and a Fossil watch for my birthday. We had only known each other for five months and he was doing a lot for me, for us to just be friends, but I appreciated it. Mike had become really jealous of our friendship and tried his best to get me back, but I wasn't going for it. I had sold my car and my truck was in the shop so Armani volunteered to let me use

one of his cars so that I could get to work, and Mike knew what two of his cars looked like. I guess Mike drove past my house that evening being nosy and noticed Armani's truck in my driveway, but my car wasn't there. He called me from his cell phone.
"Oh, you and that punk ass nigga in there laid up?"
"I'm in here in the bed."
"Yeah right, I'm about to blow this bitch up. He better come out here and get his shit."
"He's not here. He let me use his car to get to work so you better not touch his shit."
"Tell him to come get his shit. I'll take you to work."
"I don't want to get dropped off."
"Yeah, Okay." I looked out of the window and saw him walking around Armani's car.
"I'm about to call the police, you better get out of my driveway. He hung up the phone and to my surprise he left. I was happy doing what I wanted to do when I wanted to do it.

****

My Aunt Jasman belonged to this club that sponsored women with breast cancer, and they had two big cabarets twice a year to raise money and this event was my favorite because it was a two-day event. The first night we ate and drank all night for free. There was a DJ, everyone danced and socialized and the second night everyone had to wear after five's, get all dollied up and we ate a fancy dinner. There were people coming from Detroit, Chicago, Cleveland, Cincinnati and a couple of other cities for this event and afterwards they had an after party with more free food and liquor. I was so excited and couldn't wait to start my evening. I left work in a hurry that Friday evening and

I forgot my purse at work and was halfway home before I realized it. Tye was supposed to do my hair at 5:30 that evening, but by the time I found someone to open the building, got my purse and went to pick up Mikyah it was well after 6 pm. I would have left it there, but it had all my money and my ID in it. It was Memorial Day weekend and I planned on kicking it. I got to Tye's, and she had started on someone else. I wanted a quick weave because I wanted a short hairstyle, but I didn't want to cut my hair and she said it would take a couple of hours. She had her daughter start braiding my hair to the back while she put the other girl under the dryer and went to pick her boyfriend Melvin up from work. When she returned, she started on my hair and then Mikyah came downstairs looking like she had done something wrong.
"What's wrong baby?"
"Mommy, I had an accident." I looked down and her pants were soaking wet.
"Why didn't you go to the bathroom?"
"I tried but I couldn't make it." I paged Mike 911, and he called me right back.
"Do you have any clothes at your house that Mikyah can change into?" Mike only stayed around the corner from Tye and that would save me some time.
"Nope. Why?"
"Because she peed on herself and I'm trying to get my hair done."
"Oh, well no."
"Alright," I hung up and called my mom.
"What are you doing?"
"Cleaning my house."
"Can you come get Mikyah?"
"Why what's wrong?"

"She peed on herself and I'm trying to get my hair done."
"Well, aren't I supposed to watch her anyways while you go wherever you're going?"
"Yes."
"Well just bring her now. I have some clothes over here for her; I'll give her a bath and stuff."
"Okay," I hung up, went to the car, put a plastic bag on my seat and took Mikyah over my mom's. By the time Tye got started on my hair it was close to 7 pm. Mike came over when she had the back of my head done.
"Where are we going that you're getting all cute for?"
"**I'M** going to a Cabaret."
"Am I invited?"
"Not this time."
"What, your little boyfriend going with you?"
"I don't have a boyfriend and I'm going by myself."
"Yeah right," Ever since Armani had brought me a gold watch with six diamonds in it and diamond sparkles for Mother's Day, Mike had been tripping. Mike and Melvin had left and went to Mike's house to have a couple of drinks. Tye dropped them off because they usually drank a lot, and he wouldn't make it home. Tye had all my hair weaved except for the middle and we were trying to hurry up because it was after nine and she still had to cut my hair and I had to get dressed, so we weren't answering our cell phones because Mike and Melvin continued to call us, and they didn't want anything. Tye had put the last track in the middle of my head when Mike, his cousin and Melvin walked in the door.
"Ya'll couldn't answer ya'll phones?" asked Mike. He always tried to act hard around company.
"We're trying to get done." Mike walked over to the table and grabbed my cell phone and began to go through my

phone log and the phone book. I ran behind him and I tried to take my phone back, but he was bending over in a corner, and I couldn't get it.
"Give me back my phone."
"Why, what are you hiding?"
"I don't have anybody to hide anything from, so give me my phone."
"Oh, I see that nigga Armani still calling you."
"You know what, forget it, I'm calling my brother." I was walking back towards the dining room to get Tye's cell phone and Mike came running behind me.
"Call him," and he pushed me, and I feel towards the table. I put my hands out to try to catch my fall and it all happened so fast I didn't see the drinking glass sitting on the table. My hand hit the glass with so much force that the glass broke and went into my hand. I closed my eyes and took in the pain. Tye grabbed the towel that she had used to dry my hair and wrapped it around my hand because blood was gushing everywhere.
"Why the fuck did you do that bull shit? Man, give me my phone so I can go to the hospital."
"Man, ain't nothing wrong with you. You don't need to go to no damn hospital." I wasn't about to even talk to him; I grabbed my purse from the table and headed outside.
"Tye, could you call my brother?"
"What's the number?"
"I don't know, it's in my phone, just call my mom." She dialed the number and handed me the phone and it was a dead silence, I looked at the screen and the clock was still running so I waited, and Mike came outside.
"So, you still fucking with that nigga, huh?"
"Give me my fucking phone! I'm not playing."

"Fuck you!" He dialed Armani's number, and I heard him yelling.
"Meet me at our house. Yeah, you know where we live."
They continued to argue on the phone, and I got into Melvin's car with Tye. Mike heard the door shut and he ran over to the car, the window was halfway down, and Mike threw a punch through the window, but I moved, and he missed.
"Tye, go!" She pulled off and we headed toward the hospital. I hung up the phone and called my mom back.
"Mom, I'm on my way to the hospital."
"What happened?" she asked hysterically.
"Mike pushed me, and a glass went into my hand."
"Alright," I hung up and called Armani and told him what had just happened.
"Man... why do this nigga keep calling playing on my phone. There he go calling again, this is like his ninth time calling."
"Just don't answer the phone."
"I've been doing that, and he'll hang up and call right back."
"What is he saying?"
"That I better leave his bitch alone and that if I wanted to fight over you then to meet him at your house, man I don't know."
"He on some bull shit."
"I see."
"Well, I'm going to call you when I get from the hospital, if it's not too late."
"No matter what time it is, call me." Tye pulled in front of the hospital's emergency door and let me out. I went in and went to the front desk. I didn't have to say a word, I

opened the towel that was wrapped around my hand and showed the receptionist my wound. Her eyes got big.
"What happened?"
"My baby's dad pushed me, and a glass went into my hand." A nurse came over and took my blood pressure while the receptionist notified the police. She had me sit by the door to where the patients go until the police arrived and I could be the next one to see the doctor. I tried to fill out the forms, but it was my right hand that was wounded and I'm right-handed, so I gave the lady my driver's license, and my insurance cards and she filled out the forms for me, all I had to do was try to sign them. When the police arrived, they took pictures of me and my hand while Tye filled out the police report. I was so mad about getting my pictures taken because I looked a hot mess. My mom and Mikyah arrived just as I was about to go and get x-rays. She talked to Tye while I went into the back. I ended up getting six stitches and some pain pills. The female officer brought back the report that Tye had filled out so that I could sign it.
"Is this guy your boyfriend?" The officer asked.
"No, but we do things together, like go to the movies and to dinner, but we're not together."
"Well, if it's over you need to let it go, you can't do all these things with a guy you don't want to be with because some of them read into things that's not there." Thomas had told me the same thing and now I realized how right he was and why he had walked out of my life.
"I know."
"Well, if it's over, then let it be over." When I went back to the waiting room, Tye was gone, and my mom was waiting. She took me to Tye's to get my truck and from that day forward I knew I would never take Mike back.

The doctors told me that if the cut would have been two inches south, it would have cut one of my main veins and I could have died. I had a restraining order put on Mike and I stayed the night with my mom. Mike called my mom's house all night and we just let the answering machine pick it up. I had a horrible time sleeping that night with the pain, all that weave in my hair and that bandage on my hand. Sunday morning, I called and reported my cell phone stolen and they turned it off. Mike called me Monday, which was Memorial Day and talked me into dropping the charges. He gave me back my phone and some money for what he thought the medical bills may have been, and being the too nice, caring about everybody else's feelings person that I am, I went down to the police station first thing that Tuesday morning to drop the charges, but due to the severity of the case the state had picked it up and there was nothing that I could do. That Thursday Mike was pulled over for a traffic violation and was arrested because he had a warrant for his arrest. Since he was already out on bond from another case, they put a holder on him and did not give him a bond.

CHAPTER- 45

Mike was in jail for two months. Armani was a big-time dope dealer, and his houses were raided and with my luck, he and Mike were locked up together. After my continuous letter writing to the Judge, prosecutors and to Mike's Lawyer they finally let Mike out until our court date. While Mike was gone, I had run into Gabe one night at the club, he was the guy that had taken Shawn, Tina and me to dinner ten years ago, after I had found out Mike had gotten Angelica pregnant. We had started spending a lot of time together, but after I got to know him, I didn't really like him because he had a lot of drama and issues in his life that I wasn't willing to deal, but he was convenient, so I kept him around for a minute. He'd come over my house and wash my car, cut my grass, cook dinner for me and if I had just gotten off work and he was there, he'd run my bathwater. He would have been a good man if he had a job, a car, or anything to call his own or if he wasn't wanted by the police for robbing a bank, so he says. We kicked it for the whole month of July, we went to cookouts, to the clubs, to all the afterhours and all his friends showed me much love. It was not one day that I didn't have something fun to do. I never had to pay to get into the clubs and usually drinks were on them. By the middle of July Gabe had tried to move in. I started noticing clothes lying around the house and he started doing extra deeds. He had gone to the store to buy some clothes and he brought them to my house and put them in my hall closet and I packed them up for him when I dropped him off. Every day he would call and ask me to come get him and then he'd try to spend the night. I let him stay a couple of times, but he had to sleep on the couch because even though I had three bedrooms and my daughter had bunk beds, she slept with me whenever she wanted to. He kept my house clean, so I really didn't mind him being there, but I was looking for a husband and he wasn't it. I called Tye one evening because I needed someone to talk to about Gabe.

"Girl, I got to shake Gabe. I don't know if he's trying to move in or what, but he's messing up my steelow and he's got to go. I feel sorry for him, but I can't help nobody that's not trying to help themselves."

"That's fucked up, give him a chance he might get his act together. He's cool people."

"I don't want him; he needs to get on my level. I got two college degrees, my own house, a nice car and he has nothing. I don't think that I'm better than anybody, but I worked hard to get to where I am and I'm not going to let anyone that's not contributing share this with me. I am twenty-eight years old and doing damn good and when you see a nigga living up in here with me, he's going to be contributing."

"I guess so, but you're acting like a stuck up, gold digger."

"No, I'm not, I just want more out of life, and I feel I deserve it."

****

One morning Gabe and I had gotten in from the after hour around 5:30 am and he was asleep on the couch, and I was upstairs in the bed and around 8:30 I heard someone banging on my door. I looked at the clock and closed my eyes because I wasn't expecting anyone and if it was my mom she would have called first. The knocking began to get louder and then my phone rang. I looked at the caller ID and Mike's number came up. *Man, what does this nigga want this early in the morning?* I thought. I

decided that I would just let him knock and maybe he would go away. He stayed outside for twenty minutes and then I heard him on my front porch. My porch is closed in, and my outside door is always locked, so I don't know how he got onto my porch. He began to knock on my front door and then my windows and I continued to lie there. Gabe got up and came upstairs.
"Who is that at your door?"
"My baby's daddy, just let him knock, he'll leave." He lay down on the bed beside me and Mike started yelling my name.
"Kya, come open the door." I had gotten tired of him. I saw that he wasn't going to leave, I was sleepy, and he didn't have any reason to be there because Mikyah was gone. I gave him five more minutes and then I called the police.
"Nine-one-one, what's your emergency?" The operator asked.
"I have a restraining order on my baby's dad and he's outside banging on my door."
"What is his name?"
"Michael Mack."
"And what is your name?"
"Kya Walters." She verified my address.
"A cruiser is on the way. Do you need me to stay on the phone with you?"
"No, I think I'll be alright." Five minutes later I heard police sirens outside of my house.
"Kya, the police are here. Let me in!" I heard Mike moving quickly around the porch. When I heard the officer knock on the door, I got up and opened the door. The male officer was on the porch talking to Mike and the female officer came inside of the house.

"So, ma'am, what's going on?"
"He came over here about a half an hour ago banging on my door. I just went to bed three hours ago, I'm tired and I don't feel like being bothered."
"He said he wanted to see his daughter."
"Well, she's not here."
"So, what do you want to happen?"
"I just want him to leave so that I can go back to sleep."
"Well, we're going to have to take him to jail because he's not supposed to be over here."
"I don't want him to go to jail. I just want him to leave and understand that it's over."
"Did you put the restraining order on him because you were afraid of him?"
"No, it was supposed to be for twenty-four hours because I never went down to the courthouse to pursue the issue, but the judge issued it. I have written her a letter and she was supposed to be lifting it." She went outside and talked to the male officer and Mike had told him the same thing about the restraining order. She got on her radio and called in to see if what we both said was true and she was waiting for a response.
"I'll just leave, we don't even have to go through all of this," said Mike.
"I'm sorry but if it comes back that the restraining order wasn't lifted, we'll have to take you to jail."
"Like I said, I don't really want him to go to jail because we do have a child together. I just want him to leave." The female officer looked at me and then at the male officer who shrugged his shoulders.
"Alright, we're going to go ahead and let you go Mr. Mack. Do you need a ride somewhere?"
"No, I'll walk."

"Alright, I'm giving you a break and I don't want to get anymore of these calls."
"You don't have to worry about that," and Mike started walking down the street.

****

Gabe and I had tickets to go to Pittsburgh on the Gateway Clipper, a dinner cruise. I had brought the tickets because you needed a credit card to reserve them, and Gabe was going to reimburse me my money. He never did and I had a lousy time. He couldn't even afford to buy me a drink. I ended up meeting some guy on the boat and kicking it with him for the rest of the night. I had met someone else before our trip and I would have preferred for him go, but Gabe and I already had planned this. My girl and all of his boys were going and that would have been messed up, so I went ahead and let him tag along. Armani was out on bond, I called and talked to him all the way back to Akron and acted as if Gabe wasn't there and from that day forward every time he would call and ask me to come get him, I was always busy or tired.

"Kya, I need to talk to your girl Tye. Can you give me her number?" Gabe asked one evening. I gave him Tye's cell phone number and I didn't think twice about it and she called me that night.
"Gabe called me crying about how you broke his heart."
"So, did you tell him he needed to get on my level?" Tye knew about the messed-up trip we had, and she knew I wasn't feeling him.
"I didn't know how to tell him that."
"Tell him to look at how I live; I am not a hood rat. I like nice things; all my shit is brand name and I want somebody

I can do things with and don't always have to foot the bill. Then he can see what I'm into." We talked for a while longer and then we hung up. I went over Tye's house that Saturday and wouldn't you know Gabe was sitting on her porch with his suitcase. I threw my head up at Gabe as to say what's up and then I walked into the house.
"Where is your mom?" I asked Tye's daughter.
"She went to the store. She'll be right back." I called her on her cell phone.
"Oh, I see you got jokes."
"What are you talking about?"
"Why you tell me to come over here, and Gabe is sitting on your porch."
"Gabe is where?"
"Sitting on your porch."
"You are lying."
"On everything."
"I'll be there in a minute." Tye pulled up five minutes later and saw Gabe for herself.
"You brought him over here."
"No, I didn't" I said with an attitude. We all sat around and played cards until it got late. Tye kept trying to act like she was tired so I would leave, but I wasn't falling for her games. I wanted to see if Gabe was leaving, it wasn't that I cared, it was just I wanted to see if she was really dirty like that.
"Alright Tye I'm about to roll out." She tilted her head towards Gabe as to say take him too. I shook my head no and I left. The following week Gabe had moved in with Tye, she had talked Mike into getting him a job with him, she stopped calling me and every time I called her, she'd say she'd call me back. I called her two weeks later because it wasn't like her not to call me in two weeks.

"Oh, your new little boyfriend moved in and now you are acting all brand new."
"That's not my boyfriend."
"You don't have to lie to me. I told you that I didn't want him anyway and if you want my sloppy leftovers, then that's on you." She sounded like she was crying.
"Whatever, I'm about to go finish cleaning up my boys' room." I knew that was a lie, she just didn't want me to know he was there.

****

It was a Wednesday morning, and my house phone rang about 6 am. I knew something had to be wrong because not too many people had my house phone number, and everyone knew I had to get up to go to work in forty-five minutes and I like to sleep to the last second.
"Kya, this nigga is about to blow his fucking brains out." A male voice yelled frantically in my ear.
"Who is this?"
"This is Gabe, now get over here." He hung up and I rolled over thinking *how in the hell did he get my house number?* I closed my eyes, and the phone rang again. I put the phone to my ear, but I didn't say anything.
"Bitch stop playing fucking game; Mike got a gun to his head. I should have never opened my big mouth," he said while crying and he hung up. I jumped up and threw on a pair of jogging pants and a t-shirt and went into the bathroom to brush my teeth. I put Mikyah's school clothes on while she was still asleep.
"Come on baby."
"Mommy I'm tired."
"We have to go see what's wrong with your daddy." Her eyes popped opened.

"What's wrong with my daddy?" She asked with tears in her eyes.
"Go brush your teeth and let's go." She quickly brushed her teeth, and we ran downstairs to put on our shoes, and I sped to Mike's house. When I got there his mom, aunt, uncle and cousin were there. I went into the kitchen to talk to him, and he smiled at me. His eyes were bloodshot red, he could hardly keep his balance and his breath reeked of liquor.
"What are you doing, man?" I asked.
"I love you baby." He picked up Mikyah.
"Baby, I want you to know that daddy love you and you don't ever have to want for nothing, you hear me? She shook her head yes. "If something happens to daddy you have all these people to take care of you." He waved his hand pointing at everyone in the room. Mikyah's eyes filled with tears and so did mine.
"Boy quit talking to that baby like that, you're upsetting her." His aunt said. I looked on the kitchen counter and there was a bottle of pills lying there empty. That bottle was just full because I was getting his kids some cereal that Sunday when I had dropped Mikyah off so she could go to church with them, and I had looked at the bottle because I was trying to see what kind of pills he was taking, and they were pain killers. I went into the living room to tell his mom. I gave her the bottle and we went outside to talk. Then we heard all this commotion in the kitchen and we both went back into the house, Mike was throwing chairs around the kitchen and knocking things off the counter. I grabbed him.
"Mike don't do this. Look at your daughter." Mikyah was sitting on the steps with tears rolling down her cheeks. Mike looked at me and he started to lose his balance. His

eyes rolled to the back of his head, and he started falling to the floor.
"Mrs. Mack, Mrs. Mack!" I yelled. She ran into the kitchen with her brother. I was trying to hold Mike up, but he was too heavy. His uncle grabbed him, pulled him into the living room and put him in the chair. They checked his pulse; it was weak, and his breathing had become heavy.
"I think ya'll need to call the ambulance." His mom looked at me over her glasses. "I'm serious." His mom called the ambulance and I left to take Mikyah to school. I tried to hold back my tears because I didn't want to upset my baby. When she got out of the car at her school, I pulled out of the parking lot, and I lost it. I cried my heart out because I felt this was my fault. I called my mom, told her what had happed then called my job and told them I would be late. I went home to regroup and to get dressed for work and then I went back to Mike's house on my way to work but they had taken him to the hospital. I told Mrs. Mack all about Gabe, how I didn't want him anymore, how Tye took him in and forced him into Mike's life when she knew he still liked me and always talked about me.
"So, all of this is over you?" I put my head down and shrugged my shoulders. We talked a while longer and then I went to work.

    That Saturday I went to the hospital to see Mike. He had been in the intensive care unit for two days and I was really worried about him, but he was doing well, and they were ready to release him. I picked him up that Sunday when he was released.
"Kya, are you going to stay with me? I don't want to be here by myself." I understood, so I let him stay the night with me. He tried to make mends, but I wasn't in love with

him anymore. We went to court about him pushing me onto the glass, I felt that he had been through enough and I did what I had to do to get the charges dropped, and it worked. As we were leaving the courthouse, I called Mike to walk out of the police station with me so we could talk. "Look, I did this for you, but I've met someone and I'm happy. Please don't call me unless it's concerning our daughter or come around me."

"You are always trying to fuck up my day," and he walked away from me. I got into my car to go on about my day, I felt relieved and stress free. I had met this guy named Phil one night I was picking up Gabe from the club. He was cool and kept my interest, but I wasn't trying to rush into anything, and I didn't want to get my hopes up. We attended a lot of fancy outings together, always in the VIP section and he had a decent job. He didn't sell drugs, nor did he have any kids. This was what I needed, a fresh start. Although Phil and I had only known each other for four months, I erased all my rainy-day numbers out of my phone. I felt something special within him and I felt that I had finally met someone that was on my level.

   Mike came over the following week to see Mikyah. "Do you mind if I lay down with her until she goes to sleep?"

"I don't care." Mike lay down with Mikyah while I got our clothes ready for the next day, watched a couple of sitcoms and by 10 pm I was ready to go to bed.

"Mike." I shook his shoulder because he had fallen asleep. "You got to go. I'm about to go to bed." He pulled the covers back over him. "Look I'm being nice by letting you come over here, now I said you have to go," and I pulled the covers off him. He jumped up and started putting his

clothes on while I sat on the edge of the bed. He was about to walk past me, but he stopped in front of me and took off his belt. His eyes were filled with tears.
"You're going to be with me or you're not going to be with anybody."
"You think I was about to put your ass in jail the last time. Don't fuck with me!"
"Well, this time at least I'll know I'm in there for a good reason." He started wrapping the belt around his hands. I started getting scared, but I knew I had to stay calm because showing fear would only boost his actions.
"Now see this is why I don't like to be bothered with you. You need to see a psychiatrist."
"Ain't nothing wrong with me."
"That's a matter of opinion."
"You think I'm crazy?"
"Something is wrong with you." He looked at me in a pitiful way.
"I love you," and he grabbed a tighter grip on the belt. I put my chin on my chest so if he tried to wrap the belt around my neck, he couldn't choke me.
"If you love me than, why do you keep putting me through this bullshit?" He loosened his grip on the belt.
"I don't know, maybe I do need help."
"Can we talk about this later? I have to go to work in the morning and I'm really tired."
"I'm sorry for disturbing your rest. I just wanted to be with you," and he started smiling.
"Okay, call me tomorrow and we can talk." He put his belt back on, we went downstairs, and he sat in the chair. He sat there for another five minutes.
"Mike, I thought you were leaving?"
"Kya, I don't want to go."

"I'm sorry, but I'm going to bed," then he started tripping again. I went into the living room and picked the phone up from the couch to call the police. He ran into the living room and tried to take the phone from me, but I had my back turned to him and he couldn't get it, so he smacked my arm, and the phone flew across the room, hit the hardwood floor and broke. This was the second phone of mine he had broken. He saw that I was agitated, and he left.

    The next couple of weeks I tried to stay busy, everyone had told Mike that they always seen me with this light skinned dude and that I seemed so happy, and I was. Phil was the perfect man. Mikyah was out of school on Christmas break, so my mom agreed to keep her for that week, and I did everything that I had wanted to do that I couldn't because I didn't have a babysitter. Monday night was soul night at the skating ring, so I went skating. I had on a pair of fitted stretch pants with pockets down by my knee and that's where I had kept my cell phone and my money. I was skating and I couldn't feel my pager going off and they were playing the jams, so I had been on the skating floor for a good half an hour. I went to sit down and take a break because sweat was running down my face and my legs were tired. I was sitting down, and I felt my pager vibrate, I took it out of my pocket, and I had fourteen missed calls and nine-voicemail messages. I started going through my log and a lot of them were from a private number and a few of them had Mike's number on them. I knew Mike always called private, so I figured all the calls were from him. I called my voicemail and listened to my messages.
"Oh, you want to play games call me back." I pressed erase.
"So, you trying to keep me away from my daughter?

Everybody involved is going to pay for this." I saved this message.
"I hope you got a bunch of plastic because I busted out all your windows. You're going to be cold tonight." I saved that message too and as I was going to the next message my line beeped and I clicked over.
"Where the fuck is you at?" It was Mike.
"Why, what do you want?"
"Why are you playing games with me and my daughter?"
"What are you talking about?"
"Why couldn't she spend the night with me?"
"I'll bring her over tomorrow she's probably in the bed." Mike had called my mom and tried to get her to let him come and get Mikyah, but she hadn't talk to me and she knew that Mike was always on some bullshit and that would be his way to make me do what he wanted because she would be his bait.
"Where you at? I'm coming up there." He heard the music in the background, and he assumed I was at the club.
"I'm about to leave here anyways, so I'll talk to you later."
"You are going to talk to me now and tell me where the fuck you are." I hung up the phone and finished skating. When I left, I finished listening to my voicemail on my way home and on one of the messages Mike said that he would be at my house when I got there, and he was going to beat my ass when he saw me. I called Cleo and told him about the messages.
"Well, what do you want me to do?" Cleo was tired of the drama and didn't want to get involved anymore.
"I don't know."
"Well call me when you get in the house," and he hung up. I wasn't going home because I was scared, and I wasn't in the mood for any mess. I called the local police department.

"Sheriffs department, how may I help you?"
"Yes, I had a restraining order on my baby's dad, but I got it revoked and now he's threatening me, and I'm scared to go home. He said that he busted out all my windows at my house and he would be waiting for me when I got home."
"Where are you?" I told her my location.
"Just sit there, I'll send an officer to meet you. What is your address?" I gave her my address and I waited on the corner inside my car. I waited for a half an hour, and I was freezing, and I didn't have that much gas, so I kept turning off my truck. I called the Sheriff's office back and the phone rang ten times, I said forget it and I went home. I saw a police car going past my house as I turned the corner, so I figured that instead of meeting me they would just surveillance my house. I went in the house and went straight to bed with my house phone and my cell phone lying beside me. I had dozed off and I woke up to the sound of glass shattering. I picked up my house phone and there was a total silence. I grabbed my cell phone and dialed 911.
"Nine-one-one, what's your emergency?" The operator asked.
"Yes, someone is breaking into my house." I said in a whisper.
"Ma'am what's your location?"
"I'm at...." My phone beeped twice and when I looked at the screen it read "signal lost." I heard a loud bumping sound that sounded like the door, and I started crying as I dialed 9-1-1 again. I heard footsteps downstairs walking across the hardwood floor. The house was pitch black and I didn't want the perpetrator to hear me walking around, so I rolled off the bed and laid on the floor where I was out of sight. The footsteps started coming up the stairs and they

were getting closer and closer to me. I held my breath so they couldn't hear me breathe. I set my phone down so the operator could hear what was going on. I continued to hear her say hello, so I turned down the volume on the phone. *What am I going to do?* I thought. I knew I had to think fast. I always slept with a crowbar beside my bed, so I felt around on the floor until I felt it and then the hall light came on and it lit up the whole upstairs. I could see the person's feet from where I was laying, and it looked like Mike's shoes. They were walking around looking in each room and after a while I didn't see or hear them anymore. I scooted on my stomach to the bottom part of the bed so I could see more of my room, and he wasn't in there. I quietly got up with the crowbar in my hand. When I stepped out into the hallway Mike, and I were face to face. He was dressed in all black with black leather gloves and a black skull hat. He looked me in the eyes.
"I love you and I hope everybody understand," and a tear fell down his face.
"The police are on their way."
"It doesn't even matter anymore." He started walking towards me and he had a long rope in his hand. I swung the crowbar and he put his arm up to block me from hitting him in the face, it hit him on his arm, and he acted like it didn't faze him. He grabbed the crowbar, snatched it out of my hand, hit me across the head with it and I began to see stars. I started walking backwards until I hit the wall and couldn't go any further. He threw the crowbar on the floor and put the rope around my head and pulled me like an animal back into the bedroom. I was trying to pull away, but he was overpowering me, and I was still a little dazed from the blow to the head. He pushed me onto the bed and tightened the rope around my neck. I heard police sirens,

but they sounded like they were far away. I tried to grab the rope from my neck because I was having trouble breathing, but it was so tight I couldn't get it off. I continued to blackout, but I'd come right back. The next thing I remember I opened my eyes and I saw all these people in white coats moving quickly around me. I had IVs in my nose and arms and my new silk nightgown was cut up the middle. I tried to sit up because I was distraught, and I didn't know what was going on.
"Ma'am, who did this to you? We need you to lie down and relax." I lay back down and began to cry. It seemed like everything on my body hurt even my heart. I really thought Mike loved me. How could he do this to me? I was in the hospital for four days. They had security outside of my room and every two hours someone came to check on me. I never told the police that Mike was the one who tried to kill me; I just thanked God that I was still alive. I packed up our bags and Mikyah and I now stay in a different State. It's been over a year and Mikyah hasn't seen or talk to her dad. She wakes up crying in the middle of the night screaming that she misses her daddy, and it hurts me so much because I tried to make things work. I still love Mike and I probably always will, but love isn't worth my life. Maybe one day, I'll be able to tell Mikyah what really happened, and she'll understand why things are the way they are.

AFTERWARDS

So many people, men and women are killed everyday in a domestic dispute. A lot of times a person will get involved with another person who treats them like a sundae on a hot sunny day then they began to think the world of that person. Nothing that they do is wrong. When they hit you, in your mind they only did it because they love you or you began to think that maybe he/she's right, *I shouldn't have gone out with my friends although I have worked all week, taken care of the kids, kept a hot meal on the table and kept he house clean.* That's not love, its abuse and there is help available. I know that people feel as if they are in love and they're in love and they don't want to see their companion hurt or locked up because you don't want to be without them, but you must draw a line somewhere. When you leave them, you have to let go and move on, they'll try do whatever it takes to bet you back into their lives, but you have to be stronger than them, mentally. Spend time with you kids, friends and family or read a book or something. Don't go to places that they may be but do something with your time.

Everyone is not as lucky as Kya and Mike, some relationships end with one person dead and the other one still goes to jail even though you were trying to avoid that, or an innocent person may get hurt and for what? Every county has shelters, hot lines, support groups and police that can help you when you need them, that's what they are there for, use them because love is not worth your life.